Ideas in Bloom
Taxonomy-Based Activities for U.S. Studies

Phyllis P. Bray
Jeanne M. Rogers

J. WESTON
WALCH
PUBLISHER

PORTLAND, MAINE

User's Guide
to
Walch Reproducible Books

As part of our general effort to provide educational materials which are as practical and economical as possible, we have designated this publication a "reproducible book." The designation means that purchase of the book includes purchase of the right to limited reproduction of all pages on which this symbol appears:

Here is the basic Walch policy: We grant to individual purchasers of this book the right to make sufficient copies of reproducible pages for use by all students of a single teacher. This permission is limited to a single teacher, and does not apply to entire schools or school systems, so institutions purchasing the book should pass the permission on to a single teacher. Copying of the book or its parts for resale is prohibited.

Any questions regarding this policy or requests to purchase further reproduction rights should be addressed to:

Permissions Editor
J. Weston Walch, Publisher
321 Valley Street • P. O. Box 658
Portland, Maine 04104-0658

—*J. Weston Walch, Publisher*

1   2   3   4   5   6   7   8   9   10
ISBN 0-8251-2633-9
Copyright © 1995 Phyllis P. Bray and Jeanne M. Rodgers
J. Weston Walch, Publisher
P. O. Box 658 • Portland, Maine 04104-0658
Printed in the United States of America

Acknowledgments

Special thanks to Rick Koop, who allowed us to participate in the middle school training program; Jennifer Smith, who provided unique training opportunities; Sharen Lewis and Kathy LaMorte, who opened our eyes to the possibilities of using Bloom's Taxonomy; and Mary Jane Ousley, who served as a content consultant.

Thanks also to the Broward County Public Schools for the verb chart and to Kathy Steiner, Lori Nielsen, and the Secondary Outcomes Writing Team of Pasco County for the definitions of purpose.

Dedication

To our families and friends, whose love, support, and encouragement meant so much to us

Contents

Watering the Blooms: Teacher Notes and Answers for Activity Pages 75

Preface

Do you ever wonder, Why do I need to know that? Much of our time in college was spent learning theory and strategies, but not necessarily how to apply them. The learning seemed useless.

In this book, you will find a successful method of using Benjamin S. Bloom's Taxonomy of Cognitive Development to teach higher-order thinking skills. These thinking skills will help students in their roles in the twenty-first century. Students need to understand that American studies can no longer be limited to U.S. history: a broader range of learning encompassing computers, citizenship, homelessness, and other topics germane to living in the world community must be possessed by the leaders of tomorrow. The "Bloom sheets" in this book can help with instruction in these areas.

The basic outline is simple. On each reproducible page, tasks are given for each of Bloom's six cognitive levels: knowledge, comprehension, application, analysis, synthesis, and evaluation. The tasks are arranged in order of difficulty. Students are to complete the tasks according to teacher directions.

The material presented here will enable teachers of students as young as fourth graders or as mature as high school seniors to cover the whole range of social studies, approached either as whole language, cooperative learning, whole-class instruction or as independent study. The material can be easily adapted to meet the needs of any classroom, whether an intermediate ungraded classroom with full inclusion, a gifted classroom, a college-bound high school classroom, or something else.

The bulk of this book is composed of reproducible pages of activities based on Bloom and their suggested answers, but a perusal of the introductory material will reveal that this book also contains a system for developing activities that will teach thinking skills. We shall explain how to develop activity pages of your own, how to tie the pages to your plan book and objectives, and how to tie this taxonomy to other models. We also include discussion starters, teaching strategies, and tips for simplifying grading, the gathering of materials, and the like. (See "Watering the Blooms.")

If you like one of our prepared pages but find that one or more of the activities do not meet your immediate needs, feel free to clip out that material and insert a new activity of your own.

Whether you decide to start by using one of the reproducible pages ("Bloom sheets") in this book or by creating a Bloom sheet of your own, whether you are a veteran of Bloom or a novice, this book is for you.

Let yourself Bloom.

WHY YOU SHOULD BLOOM: A RATIONALE

A survey of the current research on teaching critical thinking skills reveals that the emphases seem to be on four approaches: presenting knowledge so that it is useful to the learner; working subject matter into instruction that will stimulate students' thinking; using taxonomies to identify appropriate learning activities; and creating intervention programs for teaching thinking skills.

Although there are many models that attempt to classify the ways in which people learn, think, and create, ranging from Maslow's hierarchy of basic needs[1] to Guilford's Structure of Intellect[2], we believe that the most usable, and therefore the most useful, is Bloom's Taxonomy of Cognitive Development.[3] It has several advantages over other models:

- It is widely known and used.

- It has only six categories to learn and work with. (Guilford, by contrast, has fifteen, which outline one hundred and twenty separate intellectual abilities.)

- Its category labels are familiar educational terms that cause little, if any, confusion.

- It allows the teacher either to have students progress through each of the six levels as though through a hierarchy or to cover material in random order according to the students' perceived needs or learning styles.

- It emphasizes critical thinking skills and is easily adaptable to criterion-referenced objectives.

- It readily merges with other thinking skills models and taxonomies.

- It is easily adaptable for students with identified exceptionalities such as those with specific learning disabilities or those for whom English is a second language.

Although most educators who attended college after the 1950's have had exposure to Bloom's Taxonomy, many teachers believe the taxonomy is impractical or hard to use. For this reason, they often are reluctant to explore its possibilities. It is our purpose to illustrate that Bloom's Taxonomy is user-friendly. We believe that once you see how easy it is to use and how much your students like it, you will enjoy using it and will appreciate the depth of knowledge your students exhibit.

There are many rationales for teaching thinking skills. Among the most compelling is the realization that most of the students of today will spend their adult lives working in jobs that may not even exist now. As Sizer asserts:

> *Education's job today is less in purveying information than in helping people to use it—that is, to exercise their minds. . . . Information is plentiful, cheap; learning how to use it is often stressful and absolutely requires a form of personal coaching of each student by a teacher that is neither possible in many schools today nor recognized as an important process.[4]*

Another consideration, of course, is the fact that modern course descriptions and teaching standards often require teachers to teach thinking skills and to show in lesson plans just how particular objectives accomplish such teaching. Using Bloom's Taxonomy makes that easy. Bloom is easily modified to merge well with other thinking models.

For example, if Krathwohl's Taxonomy for the Affective Domain[5] is being used, you might want to employ the correlations set forth by Eberle and Hall and cited by Schurr[6]: Krathwohl's receiving corresponds to Bloom's knowledge; responding, to comprehension; valuing, to application; organization, to analysis and synthesis; and characterization, to evaluation. The same verbs, the same tasks, can be keyed to the plan book "to encourage the development of positive attitudes, interests, and appreciation that should accompany the teaching of basic skills."[7]

If Williams's Creative Taxonomy[8] is being used, the wording of Bloom tasks may need to be modified slightly. Instead of giving an application task requiring the student to select ten key terms related to Yellow Journalism and find two ways to classify them, you can promote fluency and complexity by directing the student to list all the key terms relative to Yellow Journalism and classify them in as many ways as possible. Most synthesis activities promote flexibility, originality, elaboration, risk-taking, imagination, and curiosity. You need only to determine the creative level you wish to promote and attach the appropriate verbs.

Costa[9] points out the correlations of Bloom to other thinking skills models: Guilford's structure of intellect (p. 44), the developmental writing process (pp. 102ff), the California Writing Project (p. 215), CompuTHINK and Project IMPACT (p. 256), the Connecticut Assessment of Educational Progress (p. 281), and a broad spectrum of other models (pp. 62ff).

A list of nineteen thinking skills models grouped according to emphasis (intellectual training or reasoning, critical thinking or philosophical reasoning, and creativity and creative problem-solving) that appears in *Reach Each You Teach II* might prove

useful to those who wish a broader research base for their planning.[10]

This approach to Bloom melds especially well with Gardner's Multiple Intelligences.[11] While not every frame is touched on in every Bloom sheet, the approach is multi-framed and affords many opportunities to incorporate mathematical/logical tasks, visual/spatial tasks, musical tasks, kinesthetic tasks, and intrapersonal tasks with the more commonly required linguistic and interpersonal activities.

In addition to being compatible with other thinking models, Bloom's Taxonomy can be readily fitted to curriculum objectives or to educational outcomes. An investigation of the verb lists starting on page 7 will reveal a wide range of possible activities that can be keyed to objectives and made a part of the teacher's plan book.

Notes:

1. Abraham Maslow, *Dominance, Self-Esteem, Self-Actualization*, ed. Lowery (Monterey, Calif.: Brooks-Cole Publishing Co., 1973).

2. Mary Meeker, "A Beginner's Reader about Guilford's Structure of Intellect" (El Segundo, Calif.: SOI Institute, 1974).

3. Benjamin S. Bloom, ed.; Max D. Englehart, Edward J. Furst, Walker H. Hill, and David R. Krathwohl, *Taxonomy of Educational Objectives, Handbook I: Cognitive Domain* (New York: David McKay, 1956).

4. Theodore R. Sizer, *Horace's Compromise: The Dilemma of the American High School* (Boston: Houghton Mifflin Co., 1985), 84, 89.

5. Sandra L. Schurr, *Dynamite in the Classroom; A How-to Handbook for Teachers* (Columbus, Ohio: National Middle School Association, 1989), 68-84.

6. Ibid., 72–75.

7. Ibid., 75.

8. Ibid., 85–98.

9. Arthur L. Costa, ed., *Developing Minds: A Resource Book for Teaching Thinking* (Association for Supervision and Curriculum Development, 1985).

10. Donald J. Treffinger, Robert L. Hohn, and John F. Feldhusen, *Reach Each You Teach II: A Handbook for Teachers*, 2nd ed., rev. and expanded (East Aurora, NY: D.O.K. Publisher, 1989), 21.

11. Howard Gardner, *Frames of Mind* (New York: Basic Books, 1983).

BLOOM'S PETALS: AN ANALYSIS OF THE SIX LEVELS

Bloom's Taxonomy is a structure of six levels of cognitive development. While many educators believe it to be a hierarchy, we have found that students may have less difficulty with the synthesis and evaluation (upper) levels than with the knowledge and comprehension (lower) levels. This seems to be especially true of the right-brained, creative learner and of the learning disabled student. Despite this incongruity, much of the teaching done in the traditional classroom is geared almost exclusively to the lower levels of the taxonomy.

In order to accommodate those students who achieve better at the higher levels and to foster higher levels of cognitive thought among all students, the teacher should strive to include activities from each level of Bloom. If it is important to you that students work through the levels in order (hierarchically), we suggest that you number the tasks for independent work or that you guide the students through the steps one at a time.

As we examine each of the levels, we will list sample activities related to the theme of patriotism. We selected a few of these activities to make up the sample reproducible page (or "Bloom sheet") that appears at the end of this section.

Knowledge

The first level of learning in the cognitive domain is knowledge. Activities at the knowledge level determine whether the students know the material being studied or discussed. Can they list it, define it, recite it back? Knowledge-level activities may require specific or universal recall, restatement, or rote memory.

Knowledge activities are typically simple because they require minimal thought. Reciting the Gettysburg Address is a typical knowledge activity. Because there are so few times when we are called on actually to *know* material without also *comprehending* it, Treffinger[12] combines the knowledge and comprehension categories into one, which he calls *understanding*. We have retained Bloom's separation because we feel it's important that teachers not take for granted that students know the basics: don't ask them to compare the Magna Carta with the Declaration of Independence until you are sure they can list the key features of each. Doing so might cause them to reach unwarranted conclusions or to miss major concepts while concentrating on word differences.

Note, too, that as the material becomes more advanced, the knowledge task becomes more difficult. "List ten landmark court decisions dealing with civil rights, giving the year, the litigants, and the ruling" is a much more challenging task than "List the states that seceded from the Union," but both are knowledge tasks.

Sample knowledge activities on patriotism

Write the words to the Pledge of Allegiance and to the first verse of the national anthem.

Draw an American flag. Place on it the correct number of stars and stripes, and use the appropriate colors.

Briefly describe the two major documents on which the American system of government is based.

Retell one of the stories about the patriotism shown during the Revolutionary period (for example, Patrick Henry's "Give me liberty" speech, the Boston Tea Party, or Betsy Ross's designing the original flag).

List five or more colonial-period patriots.

Comprehension

Activities at the second level of learning determine whether students understand what they have learned. They ask the students to grasp the meaning of the material; to catalog it in their minds; to understand its significance to their needs, interests, or relationships; to personalize or internalize the material; or to interpret and translate their learning into oral, written, graphic, or nonverbal communication.

Sample comprehension activities on patriotism

Illustrate the freedoms guaranteed by the Bill of Rights.

Explain the symbolism of the American flag (its colors, the stars, the stripes, and so on).

Describe the three branches of government and the resultant system of checks and balances.

Brainstorm a list of events at which the national anthem is routinely played.

Tell how the definition of *patriotism* can be extended to include nationalism, public service, and loyalty.

Application

Activities at this level of cognitive thought determine whether the students can use the material in new ways. They ask, How could you use this? or How would you solve this? They differ from practice activities, which usually seek to test comprehension, in that they make use of the learned data in a new and different context. Knowledge must be

transferred from the arena in which it was learned to a new forum of the student's choosing. Applications often result in a product.

Sample application activities on patriotism

Assemble a collage related to patriotism.

Discover something about the life of an early patriot of your choice and describe the patriot's contribution to the establishment of the U.S. government.

With other students, role play interviews with patriots. Base your answers on the biographical research your group has done.

Determine the types of symbols and mementos owned by the members of your group and their families. Display samples for the class to view, if possible.

Construct a pamphlet to show basic flag etiquette.

Analysis

The fourth level of the taxonomy is analysis. Analysis activities break the data into component parts. They ask the students to extend the material, to relate it to previously learned material, or to draw conclusions about the material. They may require the learner to list the characteristics of a problem or situation, to look closely at the end to determine the relationship of one part to another, or to discover the relevance of the way parts are organized. They do *not* involve simple recall, summa-

tion, or restatement. At this level, the material is back in its original form without the addition of "what ifs" or changes.

Sample analysis activities on patriotism

Compare the Articles of Confederation with the Constitution. Present your findings to the class.

Conduct a survey to determine the national origins of classmates and the length of time since immigration. Make generalizations about your data.

Illustrate the gaps that exist between the knowledge that a candidate for naturalization must have about America and that which is possessed by any five native-born adults of your choice.

Draw conclusions about the patriotic effect of four American wars: the American Revolution, the War between the States, World War II, and the Vietnam conflict.

Synthesis

Synthesis activities ask the students to put the parts back together, forming them into a new product. The students will combine concepts or principles to create new information, generalizations, ideas, or feelings. A product is considered "new" if it is new to the learner and not simply a rehash of a previous experience.

The synthesis step is often omitted by teachers. It requires more time than the others. It can require extensive materials, which can be costly. The results aren't exact or predictable and are not easily evaluated. These problems should not stand in the way, however, because the synthesis step is valuable. This is the step that proves that the student has mastered the material and found a use for it: the information hasn't just been taught, it's been caught. The students who learn to synthesize information can research the data needed to solve problems and apply them as they need to. They can learn more than just what we teach them. Their vision will not be confined to the limits of our own.

Sample synthesis activities on patriotism

Cluster the results of your survey in several different ways (for example, age of respondents or country of origin) and present your finding to the class.

Imagine yourself as an American patriot in the post-Revolutionary period. How would life have been different for you?

Develop a poem or song about patriotism.

Design a handbill typical of the Revolutionary period to advertise America and its causes.

Write an essay on the theme "What America Means to Me."

Create an advertising campaign that promotes the American way of life.

Evaluation

Evaluation activities ask the students to make and support judgments about the material.

These judgments may be quantitative or qualitative value judgments; they are based on established criteria, not on opinion. Evaluation activities may also require the student to become an inventor or a creator. Evaluation activities produce the highest level of outcomes in the cognitive domain because they contain the essentials of all the other levels. For this reason, teachers sometimes choose to lead students through the entire taxonomy but to score only this level.

Sample evaluation activities on patriotism

Compare current attitudes toward revolutionaries in colonial America with attitudes toward revolutionaries today. Speculate on the reasons for the different attitudes.

Which form of nationalism do you believe is likely to be most important in the future? Give reasons for your answer.

Assume the identity of a plantation owner, a slave, a woman, a Philadelphia businessman, or an indentured servant. From that perspective, write an editorial for a colonial paper outlining the differences between your life and the ideal of liberty and justice for all.

Once you've explored the levels of the taxonomy, you are ready to begin helping your students apply them to a social studies topic. Many teachers use Bloom activity pages without ever discussing with students the terminology of the taxonomy or the thinking skills it employs. While this technique succeeds in

terms of the students' completing the required activities, it does not teach the thinking skills themselves.

Once you feel comfortable with the taxonomy, you may choose to teach it to your students, so they can understand the objectives behind the activities and can know the levels at which they are working. If you were also to post the verb list, they could write their own activity pages for subjects they wish to investigate. This is especially useful in classes where work is individualized or dispersed among small groups. The bulk of the planning can be passed from the teacher to the students, reaping a bonus both for the teacher in time saved and for the students in learning to identify a problem, to plan a means of solving it, and to implement that plan.

Notes

12. Treffinger, op. cit., 24.

Patriotism

Knowledge: Draw an American flag. Place on it the correct number of stars and stripes, and use the appropriate colors.

Comprehension: Brainstorm a list of events at which the national anthem is routinely played.

Application: Discover something about the life of an early patriot of your choice and describe the patriot's contribution to the establishment of the U.S. Government.

Analysis: Conduct a survey to determine the national origins of classmates and the length of time since immigration. Make generalizations about your data.

Synthesis: Develop a poem or song about patriotism.

Evaluation: Which form of nationalism do you believe is likely to be most important in the future? Give reasons for your answer.

HOW DOES YOUR GARDEN GROW? DEVISING, USING, AND GRADING ACTIVITY PAGES

In formulating an activity page using Bloom's Taxonomy, step one is selecting a topic. This may be a broad interdisciplinary topic (such as "change" or "power" or "relationships"), a more specific, subject-related topic (such as "causes of World War I" or "the California Gold Rush"), or a topic you intend to treat in a totally fun, affective way (such as "music videos" or "bubble gum").

How often to use Bloom is a matter of personal choice, since Bloom sheets are an extremely flexible tool intended to enhance what you teach, not to replace it. You could choose to teach an entire course using Bloom sheets, providing an experience similar to whole language instruction by doing in-depth studies of a limited number of themes. Most teachers, however, will probably use Bloom as a supplement to the curriculum they already follow. Selection of topics for Bloom sheets can be based on student interest or on your knowledge of which curriculum topics need the most coverage.

If you are going to construct your own Bloom sheets, we suggest that you start with what you already teach. Pull out a worksheet you currently use and the unit objectives that go with it. Compare the tasks with the taxonomy by looking at the verbs you use and deciding at which level these verbs appear. The verb chart on page 8 can be used to evaluate these levels.

Next, decide which levels you need to augment or add. All that remains is for you to choose the most important idea for each level, write one or more tasks to support that idea, and create your activity page, adding appropriate art or clip art if you wish.

You will probably want your activity page to include at least one activity from each level of Bloom's Taxonomy. The verb list can be used to generate these activities. Note that the verb list is not all-inclusive and that sometimes verbs appear at more than one level. For example, "Compare mail delivery by pony express with mail delivery by train" is a task that uses *compare* at the comprehension level. However, in "Compare life in the West before and after the completion of the transcontinental railroad" *compare* is used at the analysis level. There is an overlap of verb usage in the different levels. It is the *intent* of the task and not the verb itself that determines the level of the activity.

Do not spend an inordinate amount of time trying to concoct a task for each level: some overlap is natural and unavoidable.

However, the more familiar you become with the process, the more likely you will be to construct tasks at each level of the taxonomy.

The suggested list of starting phrases on pages 12–14 will give you some more ideas about how to construct your own activity pages or how to adapt the ones in this book for your use. Let's consider then the logistics of using the activity sheets and of grading them.

Using Activity Sheets

Activity sheets have a number of advantages over traditional worksheets and study questions like those typically found in textbooks. These advantages include the following:

- They are compact. These activity sheets offer a variety of tasks all on one page.

- They are attractive. The graphics are motivational in nature. According to Sizer,

Virtually all of learning comes down to incentives. I learn what I want to learn. I want to learn what I value or am convinced by people whom I trust that I will eventually value. I want to learn what is fun, what is interesting, what respected elders tell me is important, what gives me a kick, what I am good at. (Horace's Compromise 164)

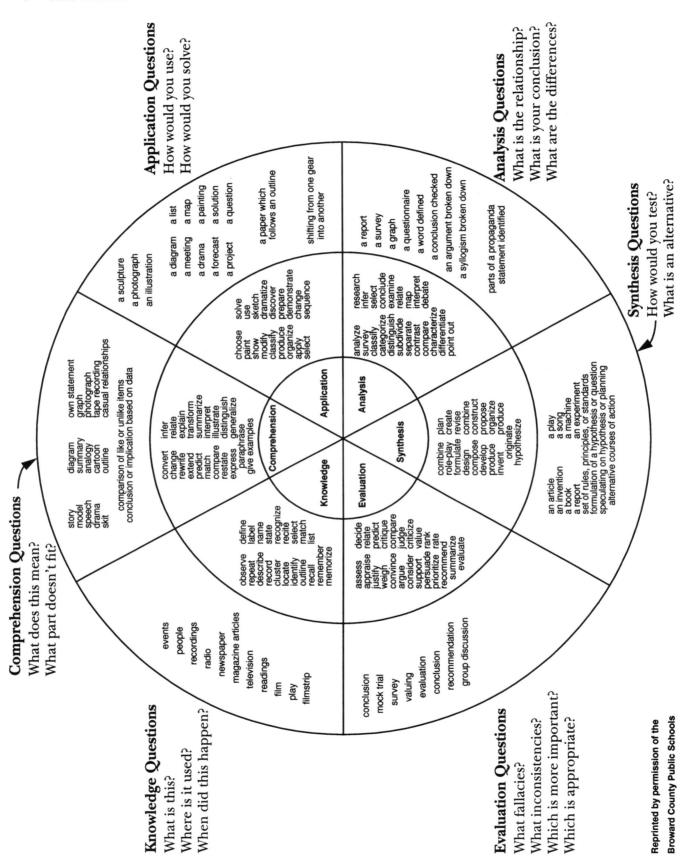

Application Questions
How would you use?
How would you solve?

Analysis Questions
What is the relationship?
What is your conclusion?
What are the differences?

Synthesis Questions
How would you test?
What is an alternative?

Comprehension Questions
What does this mean?
What part doesn't fit?

Knowledge Questions
What is this?
Where is it used?
When did this happen?

Evaluation Questions
What fallacies?
What inconsistencies?
Which is more important?
Which is appropriate?

Reprinted by permission of the
Broward County Public Schools

- They are flexible. Work may be assigned to an individual or may be done cooperatively in pairs or small groups.

- They are versatile. These activity sheets can be used as regular assignments, make-up work, learning stations, pre- and post-tests, or home instruction units.

  They may also be used as extra credit work. A student might be asked to choose among five or six activity pages and place the chosen page in a folder. When the regular work for the day is completed, the student could then work on the Bloom activities. The packet of materials produced would then become a project grade or extra credit for the grading period during which they were submitted.

- They are interdisciplinary. By their very nature, Bloom sheets draw on the student's background in science, social studies, language expression, and mathematics. Because the higher levels of the taxonomy often involve drama, art, music, and the like, the activity sheets are almost always cross-curricular with those areas. Activities that are not interdisciplinary can easily be adapted.

- They are easily organized. The student can keep track of work by coloring in the page as activities are completed and can then use the finished page as a cover sheet for the packet of written work.

- They are thought-provoking. Although you may require the students to do all six activities in order, there are other options. You may allow the students to skip around. You may allow them to do the knowledge task and any three others. You might assign point values to each level and have students complete enough items so that their total point value is 50 or 100. If you are careful in assigning the point values, you can force the students to choose from three or more categories in order to get an exact score, but you never actually have to tell them to do so. This system has the added advantage of allowing students of varying ability levels to succeed on their own terms.

Grading Activity Sheets

Grading student work requires planning, because the sheer volume of work received from each student could make grading an overwhelming task unless you look for some alternatives. We have found the following statements to be axiomatic:

Not everything has to be graded.

If the knowledge task is "select the materials that you will use to complete this page," the task is self-grading; if students can finish the activity page, they must have done this step correctly.

Grades can be based on completeness, speed, accuracy, quality, appearance, or some combination of these.

See the sample score sheet, "Images of America: Collage" The only rule is that the criteria need to be explained to the students before they begin work. When we use the collage grading sheet, we give a copy to the students on the day the assignment is made. Students are expected to fill out the top part and turn the page in with the completed project. The letter grade that the student assigns himself or herself completely controls the 20 points available for effort: A = 20, B = 15, C = 10, D = 5. Before we will accept a grade sheet with the F checked, it must be signed by a parent. If we do not receive the signed grade sheet and no project comes in, we contact the parent by telephone regarding the assignment.

One or two items can be chosen at random for grading.

Where answers are invariable, the students may be provided with an answer key and allowed to grade themselves.

Tasks may be assigned a point value, with the students' grades determined by totaling the values of the tasks they complete.

Grading may be done as a cooperative learning activity.

Students may present their work to a group of their peers (randomly chosen) who will discuss the work and reach consensus on a grade. It is important that the teacher retain veto power over these grades. Such power should be exercised only in extreme cases, such as when students exhibit an obvious bias that affects the grade. One class could evaluate another class's

Name _____ Date _____

Score Sheet: "Images of America" Collage

1. Briefly tell what kinds of pictures you selected and why you feel they are images of America. (Use the back if you need more space.)

2. About how long did you work on your collage?

3. Give yourself a letter grade, rating yourself on the effort you put into the collage.

   _____ A = I gave a lot of thought to the pictures I selected and to where I placed those pictures on the poster. I tried to get a variety of colors and topics. I searched for things that would be unusual. I tried to be neat.

   _____ B = I gave some thought to the pictures and their placement. I tried for a pleasing arrangement. I tried to be neat.

   _____ C = I took just about any picture that seemed topic-related. Mostly I was hurrying to finish.

   _____ D = I just wanted it over with.

   _____ F = I didn't do one and will not do one within the next week.

DO NOT WRITE BELOW THIS LINE

_____ Date turned in (-10/day late)   _____ Use of color (10)

_____ Full-sized poster board (5)   _____ Originality (20)

_____ Title on face (5)   _____ Effort (20)

_____ Name on reverse (5)   _____ Neatness (15)

_____ Relevance of photos (20)   _____ Montage or poster (-10) work, with the same restrictions as above. This has the added advantage of allowing work to be published to more than one group.

Other grading suggestions include the following:

- Students may create criteria against which work is evaluated.

- Students may do self-evaluations using checklists, participation charts, or rating scales.

- Students may be asked to keep anecdotal records of their progress and process; this may be graded instead of or in addition to the activity packet.

- Students may choose their best activity, place it on top, and know that only that one item will be graded provided that all the requisite items are present.

- All activities may culminate in one master product, which is then graded.

- The activity packet may become part of a participation grade, and a traditional test may be administered, with the unit grade depending on the test responses.

Note, too, that the Bloom activity page itself may be used as a test to evaluate other units of study.

Whatever you decide about grading, two things seem prudent: the product needs to meet the educational objectives set down before the tasks were designed, and the grade needs to reflect the established grading criteria (set down beforehand).

One final consideration: materials. Many of the activities in this book require brochures or other information from various organizations. In the answer key section you will find suggestions for simplifying that process, as well as addresses where applicable. However, it can be stress-producing to want to work on a Bloom sheet tomorrow or even next week only to realize that you haven't collected the materials and have no time to do so. Perhaps you would do well to hold a letter-writing lesson early in the semester and have students write to all the places whose materials you think you'll use. As materials come in, they can be filed away for later use. A perusal of the answer pages can help you compile a list of things to write for.

CUTTINGS AND SEEDLINGS: STARTER PHRASES FOR NEW ACTIVITIES

Although we find the circular chart of verbs (p. 8) to be an easy, convenient reference (which we strongly suggest you copy and place in the front of your plan book or, better yet, turn into a wall chart or bulletin board in your classroom), a longer list of verbs and some more concrete examples of activities may be helpful for those new to Bloom's Taxonomy. The following starter phrases will assist you in selecting activities appropriate to each level of the taxonomy. Remember that the levels are not discrete; they may overlap, especially in the beginning.

Knowledge

diagram and label the parts

choose the items that fit the category

recite five facts about

brainstorm a list of

list the materials used

find pictures that illustrate

acquire the meanings of

record the questions you need to answer in order to

select a game or puzzle that reinforces

count the items

identify the uses

indicate which items don't belong

write the answers to the WH questions (who, what, where, when, why, how)

fill in the chart

play the memory game

define terms

match the terms with their definitions

use the vocabulary in sentences

take the quiz

draw a mnemonic device

memorize the parts

name three types

outline the properties

alphabetize the list

recall in your group the answers to the activity questions

research your topic to discover

recognize some of the ways

repeat the computer drill/practice

reproduce the data on flashcards

trace the history of

cite examples

state your observations

complete the workbook page

read the programmed material and check your responses

search for information about

follow directions

Additional verbs:

group	underline
point (out)	copy
ask	taste
listen	quote
distinguish	know
indicate	pick
tabulate	

Comprehension

explain the procedure

summarize the main ideas or facts

rewrite as a drama

use a diagram to explain

predict the consequences

outline the implications

tell how _____ works

tutor a peer

draw conclusions

reorganize the facts on a mobile

retell in your own words

give at least five examples

define the relationship

describe the features

make inferences

suggest why

estimate the effect

list five facts and five fallacies about

expand into a news article or TV bulletin

represent the changes in

determine what trends are evident

discuss the composition

teach your group

extend into a group report to the class

show and tell

prepare a time line

convert each term to its abbreviation or symbol

illustrate with a chart or poster that shows

paraphrase the data

rearrange into a graph

express in other terms

put in order

fill in

Additional verbs

translate	group
conclude	reorder
differentiate	demonstrate
read	interpolate
measure	reword
associate	recognize
contrast	classify
trace	suggest
extrapolate	find
infer	

Application

construct a model using

put into action

select key terms and classify them

conduct an experiment

keep records

give instructions

discover ways to classify

graph data

distinguish between

apply what you know

choose case studies and react

locate information

demonstrate how to use

produce a series of problems

classify the types

put to use

collect information

suggest a procedure

construct a pamphlet to show

differentiate among

develop a news story

record observations

employ sample data to generalize

put together

trace the development

illustrate role reversal

practice through role playing

use simulations

restructure data for an ad

organize a chart

relate the results of a group product

propose a brochure

Additional verbs

calculate	expand
perform	show
operate	manipulate
participate	utilize
complete	model
predict	prove
express	derive
investigate	discuss
make	estimate
transfer	examine
find	experiment
generalize	present
interview	plan
compute	determine
convert	

Analysis

map the concepts

select a board of directors

list the attributes of

complete a logical dissection

compare with a similar one

figure out a plan of action

differentiate by listing similarities and differences

discover the ways this is like

make inferences

determine the changes caused by

infer the relationship

identify the paradox

find the implications

label the parts

point out the advantages and disadvantages

outline the material

conduct a survey

form generalizations

eliminate the unnecessary parts

draw conclusions about the effect of

generate criteria for evaluating

report on the changes that have resulted from

examine the problems with

create a web depicting

read between the lines

make deductions

put into categories

relate ideas using an idea tree

illustrate the gaps that exist

take apart

recognize the importance of

search for similarities among

deduce the benefits of

uncover the problems connected to

Additional verbs

simplify	transform
decode	divide
inspect	order
detect	diagram
discriminate	graph
break down	group
sort	criticize
observe	formulate
question	

Synthesis

design a character to serve as a mascot for

propose an original plan

devise a game

find a new use for

generate a system

change the location and make other changes to accommodate

invent a new

create a new ending

define and suggest solutions for a current social problem

combine the parts of several different examples to form a new one

predict what would happen

paint a picture

coin a new word

modify one part and predict the consequences

compose a poem or story

prepare a book jacket

develop a projection for future events

use non-recyclables to create a new product

produce a series of diagrams or drawings

put together new ways to

originate a slogan

make up a new

Additional verbs

blend	integrate
reconstruct	alter
rearrange	form
suppose	perform
deduce	constitute
present	compile
generalize	specify
document	relate
imagine	organize
build	summarize
map out	tell
derive	write
prescribe	synthesize
explain	rewrite
categorize	transmit
arrange	

Evaluation

give reasons why you would (not) recommend

make a choice

measure the success . . . tell your criteria

prepare a logical argument for or against

decide on the criteria and evaluate

do you think

evaluate the data or conclusions

explain your vote for

recommend three improvements

rank order by importance

what changes would you make if

defend your position with an editorial

grade the product, presentation, or project developed by your peers

determine the consequences

assess the limitations

use your criteria to select

pretend you had the power

judge the potential of

take a position and justify

support your stance

debate the morality of

Additional verbs

validate	distinguish
conclude	test
interpret	verify
contrast	discriminate
describe	award
choose	standardize

Name _____ Date _____

Pre-Columbian America

Knowledge: Tell how the first people might have come to America and what their lives were probably like after they arrived.

Comprehension: Map the Bering land bridge and the possible migration routes through North America.

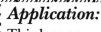

Application: Think as an anthropologist does. Write a paper in which you tell how Native American societies were changed by the coming of the Europeans.

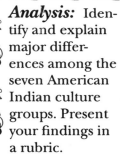

Analysis: Identify and explain major differences among the seven American Indian culture groups. Present your findings in a rubric.

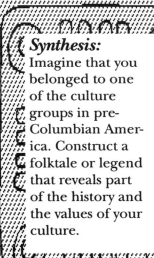

Synthesis: Imagine that you belonged to one of the culture groups in pre-Columbian America. Construct a folktale or legend that reveals part of the history and the values of your culture.

Evaluation: Decide which of the seven cultures you would have preferred to live in. Give reasons for your choice.

Name _____ Date _____

Christopher Columbus

Knowledge: List three facts about Christopher Columbus.

Comprehension: Relate the story of Christopher Columbus's discovery of America in the form of a skit.

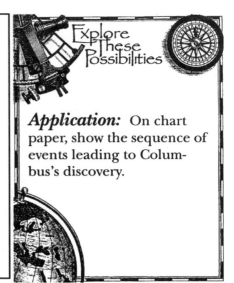

Application: On chart paper, show the sequence of events leading to Columbus's discovery.

Analysis: Research the life of Christopher Columbus and write a two-page report.

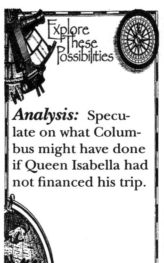

Analysis: Speculate on what Columbus might have done if Queen Isabella had not financed his trip.

Synthesis: Plan a trip to the Bahamas. What would you need to take with you if you were traveling by boat? Compare your trip to the trip Columbus made.

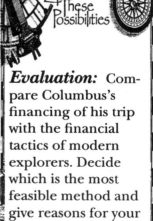

Evaluation: Compare Columbus's financing of his trip with the financial tactics of modern explorers. Decide which is the most feasible method and give reasons for your choice.

Early Explorers

Knowledge: Select three of the explorers listed below. Tell of their discoveries in North America.

John Cabot

Giovanni da Verrazano

Jacques Cartier

Martin Frobisher

Samuel de Champlain

Henry Hudson

Lewis Joliet

Robert Cavelier, Sieur de La Salle

Comprehension: Suggest reasons why there was a keen desire to find a northwest passage.

Application: Prepare a list of supplies needed for an expedition into the "unknown" territories of the North American continent.

Analysis: Suppose an efficient route to Asia from Europe had existed. What effect would that have had on the settling of the North American continent?

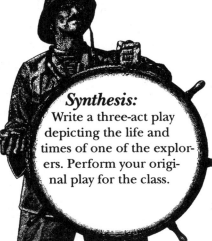

Synthesis: Write a three-act play depicting the life and times of one of the explorers. Perform your original play for the class.

Evaluation: Decide which group did the best in the following categories: script, costumes, overall performance, most historically realistic. Award the group a Certificate of Appreciation.

Ideas in Bloom

The Salem Witchcraft Trials

Knowledge: Retell the story of the Salem Witchcraft Trials.

Comprehension: Explain the cultural belief system that enabled the witchcraft accusations to be taken seriously.

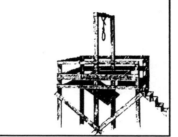

Application: Pose a series of questions that might be used by a court of inquiry investigating the witchcraft accusations.

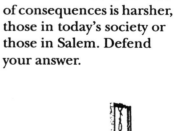

Analysis: Discover the reasons why Anne Hutchinson was accused of sorcery. Analyze the extent to which those same prejudices exist in modern society.

Synthesis: Rewrite your answer to the knowledge activity in a contemporary setting, making whatever changes might be necessary.

Evaluation: Determine the consequences in today's society of leveling false accusations. Give as many examples as you can think of. Decide which set of consequences is harsher, those in today's society or those in Salem. Defend your answer.

The French and Indian War

Knowledge: Prepare a bulletin board about the French and Indian War.

Comprehension: Write a letter to Prime Minister Pitt presenting the colonists' views on recruitment, confiscation, and quartering.

Application: Pretend you are one of the following: General Edward Braddock, General James Wolfe, or General Louis Montcalm. Write a diary entry for a day significant to the French and Indian War.

Analysis: Explain how and why the colonists prospered during (and because of) the war.

Synthesis: Speculate about how different life would be today if the Treaty of Paris had left control of Canada and the Louisiana Territory with the French instead of giving it to Britain. Write a narrative or draw a picture to show some of the significant differences.

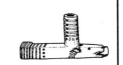

Evaluation: Examine the French and Indian War from the Native American point of view. Both the French and the English had Indian allies. With which side would you have aligned yourself? Give reasons.

Name _____   Date _____

The American Revolution

Knowledge: Identify the following: Prime Minister Grenville, Paul Revere, Crispus Attucks, the Stamp Act, the Navigation Acts, and the Proclamation of 1763.

Comprehension: Explain the slogan No Taxation without Representation.

Application: Prepare a colorful map of the Saratoga Campaign. Be sure to include a title and a legend.

Analysis: Point out three cultural differences between Britain and America that significantly affected the war.

Synthesis: Suppose that Parliament had repealed the Tea Tax and the Intolerable Acts and that war had not broken out. How would life be different if there had been no American Revolution?

Evaluation: Defend the idea that the Battle of Saratoga was the turning point of the war.

Freedom's Documents

Knowledge:
Write a one-paragraph summary of the provisions of the Articles of Confederation, the Constitution, the Declaration of Independence, and the Bill of Rights.

Comprehension:
Divide chart paper into three columns. In the outer columns, list the views of the opposing sides at the Constitutional Convention. In the center, list the compromises.

Application:
Create a constitution for your class, club, or school. Include a preamble.

Analysis:
Make a list of ways life might be different if the United States were still governed by the Articles of Confederation.

Synthesis:
Interview a signer of the Constitution. Find out what determined his state's decision to ratify. Turn your interview into a newspaper or magazine article.

Evaluation:
Tell which amendment has the most sweeping effect on your life. Explain your reasoning.

Ideas in Bloom

The Louisiana Purchase

Knowledge:
Write the answers to the WH questions (who, what, when, where, why, and how) with regard to the Louisiana Purchase.

Knowledge:
Search for information about Lewis and Clark. Write down five facts about what they accomplished.

Comprehension:
Expand your information from the two "Knowledge" activities into a news article or a TV bulletin informing the American people about the Louisiana Purchase.

Application:
Prepare a map of the United States that shows the 530 million-acre area known as the Louisiana Territory. Show the route of Lewis and Clark. Label the Ohio, Mississippi, and Missouri rivers.

Analysis: Determine the changes in United States history caused by the purchase of the Louisiana Territory.

Synthesis:
Design a character to serve as a mascot for the Lewis and Clark Expedition.

Evaluation:
Explain your vote for Thomas Jefferson in the presidential election of 1804.

Ideas in Bloom

California Missions

Knowledge: Outline information about Father Junipero Serra.

Comprehension: Give examples of Spanish influence that still exist in our society today.

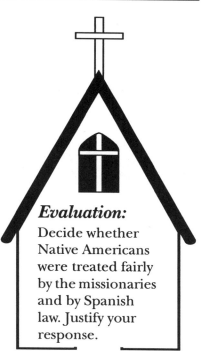

Application: Find ways in which the missionaries positively affected the lives of Native Americans prior to 1800.

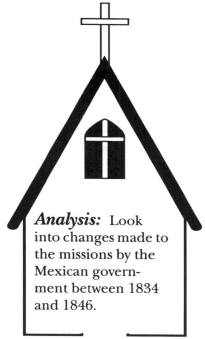

Analysis: Look into changes made to the missions by the Mexican government between 1834 and 1846.

Synthesis: Design a poster as an advertisement for a book about Father Junipero Serra.

Evaluation: Decide whether Native Americans were treated fairly by the missionaries and by Spanish law. Justify your response.

Ideas in Bloom

The Trail of Tears

Knowledge: Identify each of the following in terms of the practice of Indian removal:

Manifest Destiny
Wendell Phillips
Henry B. Whipple
James M. Cavanaugh
Sequoyah
Andrew Jackson
Martin Van Buren
General Winfield Scott
Indian Removal Act
Treaty of Tellico

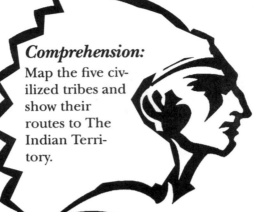

Comprehension: Map the five civilized tribes and show their routes to The Indian Territory.

Application: Before native Americans had a written language, their history was passed on in oral sagas and hieroglyphic wampum belts. Discover three or more native tales and list some of the things that were important to Native Americans as revealed in their folklore.

Analysis: Compare the Cherokee to a plains tribe such as the Apache or the Sioux. Decide why the Cherokee tribe was called "civilized" and the other wasn't.

Analysis: List things the Cherokee did to try to hold on to their tribal lands. Theorize why these actions were unsuccessful. Present your findings in a written format.

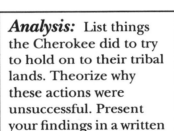

Evaluation: The Cherokee Indian Removal Act was a clear example of the breakdown of America's checks and balances system. Decide who was the more civilized—the Cherokee or the United States. Support your decision.

Synthesis: Speculate on how a governmental structure might have made it easier for the Cherokee to resist encroachment by the white man. Present your ideas on a poster or chart.

Ideas in Bloom

Name _____ Date _____

The Mexican War

Knowledge: Map the disputed territory of Texas, being sure to label the Nueces, Guadalupe, and Rio Grande rivers and to plot Santa Anna's route, Urrea's route, and Houston's route. Mark the location of the Alamo and of the battle of San Jacinto.

Comprehension: Write the script of a political debate between Clay and Polk on the issue of Manifest Destiny. Enlist the help of a classmate to present your skit to the class.

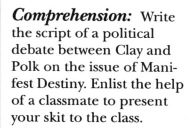

Application: You are an abolitionist angry over the possible acquisition of another slave state (Texas), over "Mr. Polk's War," over the Alamo. Design a "Wanted" poster calling for President Polk's arrest for "war crimes."

Analysis: Design a poster showing the terms of Slidell's proposal and the terms of the Treaty of Guadalupe-Hidalgo. Other than the loss of life suffered, what did Mexico lose by refusing to meet with Slidell?

Analysis: Make a sketch or model of the Alamo. How does this American fort compare to a medieval castle? Theorize as to why Americans built forts instead of castles. Present your findings to the class.

Synthesis: Design a war monument honoring either the 187 Americans or the 1,550 Mexicans who died during the 13-day siege of the Alamo. Include an "inscription" explaining why these men are being honored.

Evaluation: William Barrett Travis, Jim Bowie, and Davy Crockett were heroes long before they came together in San Antonio. Evaluate what you know or can learn about these three men and decide which was the greatest hero. Support your choice in a paper or on a poster.

Ideas in Bloom

Name _____ Date _____

The Gold Rush

Knowledge: Describe the events leading up to the discovery of gold in California. Be sure to include information on James Marshall and John Sutter.

Comprehension: Explain what a secret is and how to keep one. Suggest reasons why the men involved in the gold discovery could not keep a secret.

Comprehension: Suggest reasons why the population of California in 1848, approximately 800, grew to 25,000 in 1850.

Application: Prepare a pantomime depicting panning for gold.

Analysis: Research what happened to John Sutter after his initial discovery. Did he live "happily ever after"? Explain.

Synthesis: Suppose you were eager to reach the gold mines of the West. Consider the three major means of travel available to reach your destination. Which method would you choose, and why?

Evaluation: Criticize the greed evident during the gold rush of 1849. Include your opinion about the cost of food and supplies, as well as the disregard for the land.

Ideas in Bloom

Communication

Knowledge: Match the following inventors with their inventions:

Alexander Graham Bell
Cyrus Field
Richard Roe
Samuel F. B. Morse

rotating printing press
telephone
magnetic
  telegraph
ocean floor
  cable

Comprehension: Rearrange the inventions in the "Knowledge" box in chronological order.

Application: Locate a list of the signals Samuel F. B. Morse used in the Morse code. Create a message using the code. Exchange with a classmate and translate each other's messages.

Analysis: Determine the benefits of the telegraph.

Synthesis: Invent a new means of communication for the twenty-first century. Include a drawing or a description and an explanation of how it works.

Evaluation: Grade the inventions developed by your peers. Base your decision on creativity and thoroughness.

The Underground Railroad

Knowledge: Read a biography of Harriet Tubman. In a group with two or three others, list as many facts as you can recall.

Comprehension: Using your knowledge list, cluster the facts under two headings: the Underground Railroad and Harriet Tubman.

Application: Investigate the major route(s) traveled by "passengers" on the Underground Railroad. Trace the route(s) on a map of the northeastern United States.

Analysis: Two major analogies were employed in naming the slaves' escape mode: the routes' being called "the Underground Railroad" and Harriet Tubman's being called "Moses." Illustrate the parallels evident in these analogies.

Synthesis: Compose a sentence that presents the philosophy that spawned the Underground Railroad and guided people like Harriet Tubman. Then reduce your own guiding philosophy of life to one sentence.

Evaluation: Prepare oral arguments for debate on one side of the following topic: People have a moral obligation to break immoral laws.

Evaluation: Compare Harriet Tubman's contribution to the freedom movement with that of any four other leaders of movements. Decide which of the five was most influential or important. Make a presentation in which you justify your choice.

© 1995 J. Weston Walch, Publisher

Ideas in Bloom

The Civil War

Knowledge: Describe the events leading up to the Civil War.

Comprehension: Explain how the Civil War ended. Include names of those involved, locations, and other specific details.

Application: Choose three of the following and describe their roles in the Civil War: General Ulysses S. Grant, General William T. Sherman, General Robert E. Lee, Jefferson Davis, Abraham Lincoln, General Thomas J. Jackson.

Analysis: Select five to ten key events of the Civil War and show them on a time line.

Synthesis: Tell what might have happened had Abraham Lincoln not been shot.

Evaluation: Research the assassination of Abraham Lincoln and debate the fairness of what happened to Booth, to the other conspirators, and to Dr. Samuel Mudd.

Ideas in Bloom

Abraham Lincoln

Knowledge: Read a biography of Abraham Lincoln.

Knowledge: List ten major accomplishments of Abraham Lincoln.

Comprehension: Enlist the help of classmates to dramatize an incident from Lincoln's life. In your introduction, explain the significance of the incident.

Application: Produce a pamphlet that shows the issues facing Lincoln as he assumed the presidency.

Analysis: Lincoln's life was full of irony and paradox, but the incidents that have received the most attention involve the remarkable resemblances to John F. Kennedy's life. Chart the parallels between the two presidents.

Synthesis: Speculate on how Reconstruction might have been different had Lincoln not been assassinated. Give at least five ways in which things would have been different.

Evaluation: Lincoln overcame poverty, obscurity, and lack of formal schooling to become one of America's most revered presidents. List in order of importance the eight to ten factors you feel were most responsible for his success. Give reasons for your choices.

Ideas in Bloom

Reconstruction

Knowledge: Generate a list of problems facing Americans after the Confederate surrender at Appomattox Courthouse. On a chart, combine your list with that of classmates.

Comprehension: Assume the role of a newly freed person who has traveled to Abilene to start a new life. In a series of letters to *and from* your mother who is still in Mississippi, describe what life is like for African Americans both in the West and in the South. Be sure to write your letters in first person.

Application: Using overlapping circles, draw an illustration of the major plans for reconstruction: the Presidential (Ten Percent) Plan, the Wade-Davis Bill, the Reconstruction Act, and Johnson's Plan (Presidential Restoration Plan). Use the overlapped area to illustrate any points these plans had in common.

Analysis: Explain why rebuilding after the War between the States was so much more massive a project than rebuilding after other wars. Give at least five reasons.

Synthesis: Compose a skit, song, poem, or story about the scalawags and carpetbaggers.

Evaluation: Estimate the effects of a half century of American life under *Plessy v. Ferguson* and the effects of *Brown v. Board of Education of Topeka*. Which ruling do you believe was the more significant? Give reasons. How might life be different today had the "separate but equal" principle never been in place?

Ideas in Bloom

Westward, Ho!

Knowledge: Read a biography of an American trailblazer. List eight facts that make him or her important as a trailblazer.

Comprehension: On a map, label each of the following trails and, where possible, the explorer who opened it: El Camino Real, the Chisholm Trail, the Trail of Tears, the Oregon Trail, the Natchez Trace, the Cumberland (National) Road, the Santa Fe Trail, the Spanish Trail, the Butterfield Overland Mail Route, the Mohawk Trail, the Wilderness Road, and the Goodnight Loving Trail.

Application: With two or three classmates, draw up a list of problems you might encounter on a trip west in 1872. Decide what supplies you would need in order to be prepared for these eventualities.

Analysis: List similarities and differences between Western trailblazers and world explorers such as Marco Polo and space explorers such as Neil Armstrong and Sally Ride.

Synthesis: Examine some of the folk heroes, tall tales, and legends that arose during the westward expansion of our nation. Create a new character and write some tall tales about him or her. Use this person's exploits to explain physical features of the land or natural phenomena.

Evaluation: Investigate the importance to westward expansion of gold, free land, Indian relocation, religious oppression, civil war, industrialization, and the open range. Rank these in order from most influential to least influential. Give reasons for your choices.

Ideas in Bloom

Cowboys

Knowledge: Define the following: chaps, lasso, rodeo, wrangler, trail drive, bandanna, poncho, sombrero, Western saddle.

Comprehension: Describe what life was like on the open range.

Application: Prepare a presentation that gives five or more facts about the life of a well-known cowboy.

Analysis: Illustrate a scene in the West of 1800.

Analysis: Compare the cowboy as he is portrayed in your social studies text with the cowboys who appeared in fictional stories or in television programs and movies. What conclusions can be drawn from your comparison?

Synthesis: Create a poem, skit, or rap song about the cowboy.

Evaluation: Defend today's use of trucks, jeeps, and even helicopters to round up cattle instead of the traditional use of horses.

Ideas in Bloom

Indians

Knowledge: List the five American Indian tribes that actively participated in the Civil War. Discover whether these tribes still exist today.

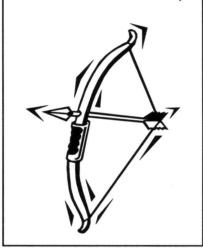

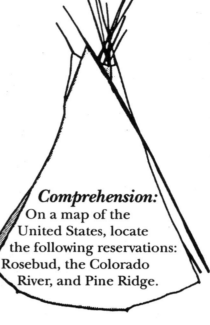

Comprehension: On a map of the United States, locate the following reservations: Rosebud, the Colorado River, and Pine Ridge.

Application: Make a replica of an Indian village.

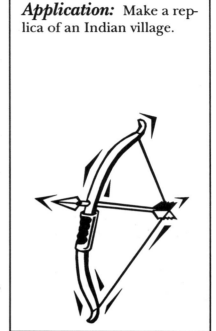

Analysis: Contrast the life of a Native American living on a reservation now with reservation life in the 1800s.

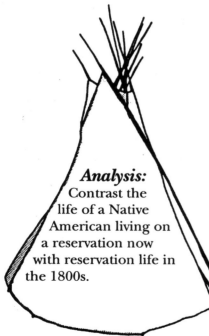

Synthesis: Predict what life would be like for Native Americans if they had not been made to live on reservations.

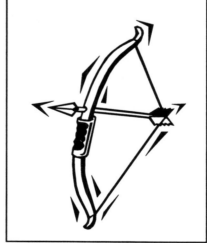

Evaluation: Describe life as you see it for the Native American in the next century.

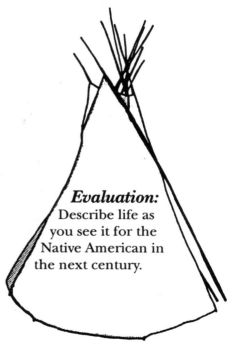

Ideas in Bloom

Western Outlaws and Lawmen

Knowledge: Identify the following: Jesse James, Billy the Kid, Sam Bass, William B. Masterson, Wyatt Earp, Patrick Floyd Garrett, and Wild Bill Hickok.

WANTED!

Comprehension: Organize the facts from the knowledge activity on a mobile.

Application: Locate information on "dime novels." Record your findings as a television commercial or radio announcement.

WANTED!

Analysis: Examine the terms *cattle rustler, train robber, hired gun, confidence man, cardsharp, claim jumper,* and *pickpocket.* Form generalizations about the character of a western outlaw.

Synthesis: Design a "Wanted" poster for a fictitious outlaw. Include the facts necessary to inform the public about this person.

WANTED!

Evaluation: Decide if it is right to "take the law into your own hands." Support your decision with a minimum of three reasons. Express your opinion in a short essay.

WANTED!

Evaluation: Decide if you are for or against the death penalty. Support your decision.

Ideas in Bloom

Name _____   Date _____

The Transcontinental Railroad

Knowledge: Find the names of three railroad lines in the United States (past or present).

Comprehension: Trace on a map the development of the Transcontinental Railroad. Where did the lines meet?

Application: Discuss the improvements made to railroad comfort and safety by George Pullman and George Westinghouse.

Analysis: Compare life in the West before and after the completion of the Transcontinental Railroad.

Synthesis: Create a railroad scene. Turn a shoebox into a railroad car. Use toothpicks or popsicle sticks to create the railroad track. Use your imagination!

Evaluation: Decide if train travel is still a useful form of transportation. Justify your decision with three reasons.

Ideas in Bloom

The Industrial Revolution

Knowledge: Write a brief paragraph telling how each of these men contributed to the Industrial Revolution: Samuel F. B. Morse, Francis Cabot Lowell, Robert Fulton, Samuel Slater, and Eli Whitney.

Comprehension: Research American demographics in 1800. Use that information to write a paragraph describing what American life would have been like without industrialization.

Application: Illustrate and label a machine that figured prominently in the Industrial Revolution.

Analysis: Working with a partner, plan a presentation to explain the effects on slavery of the invention of the cotton gin. Join another pair and take turns teaching the group.

Analysis: The development of the microchip has been cited as the beginning of a new industrial revolution. Use a graphic organizer to show how the shift from manual to mechanical labor was both like and different from the shift from industry to technology and robotics.

Synthesis: Despite the changes brought by assembly lines, interchangeable parts, and other signs of mechanization, there still are those who enjoy making products the old-fashioned way. Find an artisan in your area and interview him or her in person or by telephone or letter. Explain to the class the artisan's views on his or her product.

Evaluation: Decide whether Slater's construction of a spinning jenny was ethical in light of England's industrial secrets law. With your classmates, stage a mock trial and present your views.

Immigration

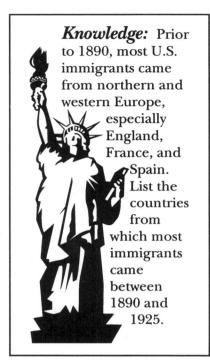

Knowledge: Prior to 1890, most U.S. immigrants came from northern and western Europe, especially England, France, and Spain. List the countries from which most immigrants came between 1890 and 1925.

Comprehension: Give three reasons why people wanted to emigrate.

Application: Locate information about either Ellis Island or the Statue of Liberty. Summarize your findings and be prepared to share with the class.

Analysis: Predict the consequences if there were no limits set on immigration.

Analysis: Point out the advantages and disadvantages of having been a newcomer to the United States. Are these advantages and disadvantages different today than they were at the turn of the century? Support your answer.

Synthesis: Suppose you are a newcomer to America. Write a report in journal form outlining your travels. Be sure to include difficulties experienced.

Evaluation: Do you think our nation was built by immigrants and their descendants? Explain.

Name _____   Date _____

Yellow Journalism

Knowledge: Define *yellow journalism.*

Application: Clip a news story from the daily paper and turn it into a piece of yellow journalism.

Application: Collect information about another important journalist of this era and tell what contributions that person made to the changing face of journalism.

Comprehension: Explain the relationship to yellow journalism of each of the following:

Joseph Pulitzer
William Randolph Hearst
the Yellow Kid
Richard Felton Outcault
Richard Harding Davis
the Spanish-American War
the New York *World*
the New York *Journal*
"Hogan's Alley"
George Luks
Frederic Remington

Analysis: Identify several common propaganda techniques, including bandwagon, name calling, card stacking, and transfer. Using newspapers, magazines, or other format, provide an example of each. Tell how each might have been used by yellow journalists reporting on the Cuban rebellion.

Evaluation: Weigh what you see as the power of newspapers to influence events during the Spanish-American War against what you see as the power of today's media to influence world events. Make a case for or against the need for legislation requiring responsible, ethical journalism.

Synthesis: Design the front page of a newspaper in the style of yellow journalism.

Evaluation: Theodore Roosevelt referred to the Spanish-American War as "a splendid little war." Give reasons why many Americans in 1898 would have agreed with him.

Name _____   Date _____

Annexation of Hawaii

Knowledge: Arrange the following in chronological order:

American residents in Hawaii revolt

Hawaii becomes the fiftieth state

Missionaries arrive in Hawaii

Queen Liliuokalani gives greater power to native Hawaiians

Territorial status is granted to Hawaii

Midway Islands are annexed

Comprehension: Explain why Hawaii was referred to as the "crossroads of the Pacific." Make a map of Hawaii to demonstrate your response.

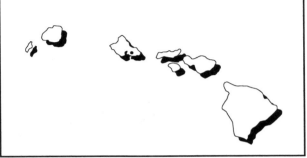

Application: Investigate what people in the 1800s believed were the pros and cons of annexing Hawaii. Organize your findings in a chart.

Analysis: Determine the effects of the McKinley Tariff Act of 1890 on Hawaii.

Synthesis: Suppose the United States had been unsuccessful in annexing Hawaii. How would this have affected trade?

Evaluation: Criticize the actions of the American residents of Hawaii in 1893. Was the role they played in the revolt against the queen justified? Explain.

World War I

Knowledge: Describe the terrorist activity in Sarajevo that is generally thought to have precipitated World War I.

Comprehension: Color a map of Europe to indicate which nations were part of the Central powers, which were part of the Allied powers, and which were neutral.

Application: Write an editorial that might have appeared after the sinking of the *Lusitania*. In it, urge the United States to join or stay out of the Great War.

Analysis: Make a poster showing how World War I was good for certain groups in America.

Synthesis: Design a recruitment poster that might be used effectively to encourage war efforts today.

Evaluation: Rank President Wilson's Fourteen Points in order of importance to America. Give a rationale for your order.

The Roaring Twenties

Knowledge: Name the president who held office from August 3, 1923, to March 4, 1929.

Knowledge: Describe the "good times" of the 1920s.

Comprehension: Explain why the decade 1920–1929 was called "The Roaring Twenties."

Application: Find reasons why the United States was so prosperous during the 1920s.

Analysis: Explain the risks associated with buying items on credit.

Synthesis: Originate a slogan that represents life in the 1920s. Display your slogan on a banner or poster.

Evaluation: Prepare a logical argument for or against Prohibition.

Ideas in Bloom

Name _____   Date _____

The Great Depression

Knowledge: Create an artifact kit about the Great Depression. Work with classmates to set up a display for the school to see.

Comprehension: Chart the alphabet agencies of the Depression era. Give the name of the agency, the date it was established, its purpose, and its resolution (whether it still exists, whether it merged with another agency, and so on).

Application: Despite both the Depression and the Dustbowl in the South-west, there were some enjoyable activities: the movies, the comics, the Big Bands, and radio's Golden Era. Illustrate one such aspect of life in the Thirties.

Analysis: Contrast the effects of the Depression on various segments of society—for example, city business owners, labor workers, southern tenant farmers, Oklahoma sharecroppers, and California migrant workers.

Synthesis: Hoover's response to the Depression was inadequate at best, and he was widely criticized for his refusal to establish direct federal aid. Yet Roosevelt's establishment of a national program has been condemned by those who say government aid destroys initiative and promotes helplessness. Working with one or two other students, generate a list of other solutions that might have been tried.

Evaluation: Americans had no lack of heroes during this era. Speculate on why hard times would produce so many heroes. Decide which kind of hero would have had the most influence on you. Give at least three reasons for your choice.

Name _____ Date _____

World War II

Knowledge: Tell the major role played by each of these men in World War II: Joseph Stalin, Winston Churchill, Benito Mussolini, Adolf Hitler, Emperor Hirohito, Franklin D. Roosevelt, and Harry S. Truman.

Comprehension: Give examples of ways in which women helped the war effort.

Application: Interview a family friend or relative who served during World War II. If possible, examine photographs taken during that time period. Prepare a written report of your meeting.

Analysis: Survey members of your class to see if they agree or disagree with the use of the atomic bomb on August 6, 1945. Graph the results using a bar graph or a circle graph.

Synthesis: Choose one: Compose a poem regarding World War II, create a poster to encourage people to enlist in the armed forces, or write a letter to the folks at home from a soldier in the war.

Evaluation: Consider the results of your survey from the analysis activity. What recommendation would you have made to the president regarding the bombing of Japan? What arguments would you present to support your recommendation?

Ideas in Bloom

The United Nations

 Knowledge: Describe the reasons for creating the United Nations.

 Knowledge: List the six branches of the United Nations.

 Comprehension: Describe the role of each branch of the United Nations.

Application:
Draw a chart or diagram that shows the six branches of the United Nations.

Analysis: Determine how FDR's Four Freedoms and Woodrow Wilson's Fourteen Points influenced the United Nations. Write a report stating your findings.

Synthesis:
Design a plan for world peace. Share your plan for peace through a skit, a poem, or a song. Be specific and include a set of rules and standards.

Evaluation:
Decide if it is necessary to have United Nations peace-keeping forces. Justify your opinion with three reasons.

Communism

Knowledge: Use a time line or flow chart to show, by nation, the spread of Communism from the Bolshevik Revolution in 1917 to the present. Color code your entries to distinguish those nations that are no longer Communist from those that still are Communist.

Comprehension: Explain the three key Communist concepts of historical materialism, dialectical materialism, and economic determinism.

Application: Work with others to produce a mural depicting life under Communism in the Soviet Union.

Analysis: Investigate one of the American socialist Utopian projects. In what ways was it similar to Marxist-Leninist Communism? How was it different?

Synthesis: Produce a skit or role-play that presents one person's experience with the fall of the Berlin Wall or with the fall of Soviet Communism.

Evaluation: Attempts to achieve communal societies have been as massive as Soviet Communism and as limited as the Cedar Vale Community, as apolitical and unstructured as Haight-Ashbury and as rigid and sectarian as Jonestown. List seven to ten reasons why most of these ventures have failed. Make another list of things you think are necessary for a society to survive.

Ideas in Bloom

The Korean Conflict

Knowledge: Create a historical marker commemorating an event during the Korean Conflict relative to one of the following:

the United Nations
the Soviet Union
Red China
the Cold War
the 38th parallel
Harry S. Truman
Dwight D. Eisenhower
Douglas MacArthur
Joseph Stalin
Joseph McCarthy

Base your decisions about what to include on what you know or can find out about historical markers.

Comprehension: Do a RAFT writing assignment that summarizes the Korean Conflict.

Application: Create a storyboard to retell the major events of the conflict. Include an interesting opening, six "cliffhangers" (for fade-to-commercials), and a satisfactory closure.

Analysis: Compare the isolationist policy of the United States after World War I to its policies after World War II, including the Marshall Plan, the Korean Conflict, and SEATO. Decide what caused this shift of focus. Present your ideas to the class.

Synthesis: Revise your RAFT writing, changing one major factor and predicting how that change would have affected the course of the conflict.

Evaluation: Make a decision scale weighing the advantages and disadvantages of having a civilian (the president) in charge of the military. Put the pros on one side and the cons on the other. Decide as you go if some of the items should weigh more (be bigger) than others. Tilt the top of the scale to show if it balances in favor of the pros or the cons.

John F. Kennedy

Knowledge: Assume the role of a biographer about to interview Kennedy in the summer of 1963. Because he is such a busy president, you will be allowed to ask only ten questions. Make a list of the questions you will ask and supply his probable answers.

Comprehension: Kennedy was America's first Catholic president. Discuss why his religion was a campaign issue.

Application: Make a record book listing the accomplishments and failures of Kennedy during his term of office. If possible, include quotes, pictures, and anecdotes.

Analysis: One of the ways to tell what a person is like is to look at the person's heroes. Kennedy wrote about some of his heroes in a book called *Profiles in Courage*. Read one of the profiles and tell how Kennedy was like the person profiled. What challenge did the person meet? What was the result?

Synthesis: Suppose that Kennedy had not died in Dallas. Make a list of outcomes that might have resulted from his finishing his term of office.

Evaluation: Kennedy is generally credited with five major accomplishments: proposing significant civil rights legislation, establishing the Peace Corps, providing support for the manned space program, patronizing the fine arts, and supporting an atomic test ban. Of these five, which do you think was most important? Why?

Name _____ Date _____

The War in Vietnam

Knowledge: Explain the Tonkin Gulf Resolution and how it differed from a congressional declaration of war.

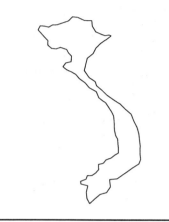

Comprehension: Although the war in Vietnam had been going on for twenty years when Lyndon Johnson took office and America's policy on containment of Communism dated back to the Eisenhower administration in the late 1950s, Johnson took most of the blame for the war in Vietnam. Explain how the actions Johnson took caused him to be blamed.

Application: Write an editorial in which you take the position of a 1960s hawk or dove and express your opinion on American involvement in the Vietnam War.

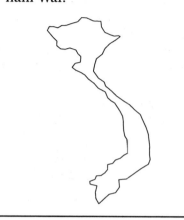

Analysis: The Vietnam War was fought for the same principles that had precipitated the Korean Conflict, yet it met with little of the popular acceptance evident during the Korean Conflict. Make a chart or diagram that compares the two hostilities and try to account for the differences in perspective.

Synthesis: Create a display featuring the counterculture that grew out of the disillusionment of youth with the dominant culture of the 1960s and its participation in the Vietnam War. Include clothing, hairstyles, music, language, art, fads, and so on in your display.

Evaluation: Explain how America achieved (or did not achieve) "peace with honor" in Vietnam. Base your conclusions on your study of Vietnam.

Ideas in Bloom

The Green Berets

Knowledge: Briefly tell how the U.S. Special Forces came into being.

Comprehension: Explain how guerrilla warfare differs from combat.

Application: Make a "Mobile of Fame" having at least five shapes on which you have mounted facts about ten Green Berets.

Analysis: Although there were other irregular warfare forces established after World War II, the Green Berets achieved more recognition than other groups such as the navy's SEAL teams or the air force's Air Commandos. Compare the work of these three special forces and draw a conclusion about why the Green Berets were so well known.

Synthesis: Compose a song or poem expressing your feelings about some aspect of warfare or the military.

Evaluation: The Green Berets' medical teams worked not only on curing falciprium malaria, tropical sprue, and other diseases that affected soldiers, but also on treating leprosy in and providing inoculations for civilians. Consider whether the good that they did outweighed their mortality rates and whether they were a necessary part of the war. Argue your conclusions in an editorial, giving support for your arguments.

Ideas in Bloom

The Civil Rights Movement

Knowledge: Read the Bill of Rights. Select three of these amendments and list the rights they guarantee to all Americans.

Comprehension: Explain what is meant by "separate but equal."

Application: Learn the important dates in the civil rights movement and show them on a time line.

Analysis: Point out the significance to the civil rights movement of the Thirteenth Amendment, the Supreme Court decision in *Brown v. Board of Education of Topeka*, and the Civil Rights Act of 1964.

Synthesis: Working with a partner, make a list of five rights to which all people are entitled regardless of race or religion.

Evaluation: Rank your list of five rights, placing the most important one first. Justify your choices.

Evaluation: You are responsible for developing a new code of conduct for your school. Determine the rights that should be guaranteed to all students.

Martin Luther King, Jr.

Knowledge:
Read a biography of Martin Luther King, Jr. Find pictures that represent at least ten significant events in his life. Organize them on a poster or collage or in a scrapbook.

Comprehension: Locate and read the text of three of Martin Luther King's statements or speeches. Write a one-sentence summary of the main idea of each.

Application:
Locate the lyrics of three to five songs important during the civil rights movement, including "We Shall Overcome." Explain their significance to the movement.

Analysis: Compare King's "I Have a Dream" speech with Langston Hughes' poem "I Dream a World." How are they similar? How different? What other evidence can you find to show how black authors influenced King?

Synthesis: Write a play, poem, or essay about overcoming prejudice.

Evaluation: Report on the contribution to the civil rights movement of another individual of your choice. Decide how that person influenced, or was influenced by, King. Justify your answer.

Space Exploration

Knowledge: Search for information about why satellites stay in orbit. Present your findings on a poster or chart.

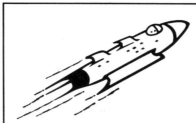

Comprehension: Prepare a time line having at least ten events that are significant in the history of space exploration.

Application: Trace the development of NASA from the end of World War II to its establishment by law on July 29, 1958.

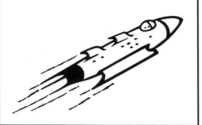

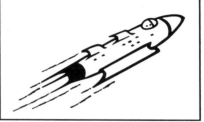

Analysis: Examine the roles of natural resources, economic prosperity, highly developed technology, and massive land areas in the space race. From your data draw conclusions about why other nations did not participate in the race to the moon.

Analysis: The first Soviet woman in space made her historic flight twenty years before NASA sent a woman into space. Make a list of cultural differences that might account for this disparity.

Synthesis: Develop a projection of future events in America's space program.

Evaluation: The destruction by fire of *Apollo 1* and the 1986 explosion of a *Challenger* STS cost the lives of ten U.S. space explorers, including two who were not traditionally trained astronauts. Decide whether the advancements afforded by the space program are sufficient to justify this loss of human life. Defend your position in an editorial.

Ideas in Bloom

Airplanes and Automobiles

Knowledge:
Place each of the following names under the heading Airplanes or Automobiles: Henry Ford, Charles A. Lindbergh, Charles E. and J. Frank Duryea, Glenn H. Curtiss, Jacqueline Cochran, and Frances E. and Freelan O. Stanley.

Comprehension:
Explain the contribution each person in the "Knowledge" box made to either the automobile or the airline industry.

Comprehension:
Explain the term *barnstormer.*

Application: Choose one of the following activities.

a. Sketch an automobile or an airplane.
b. Construct a model car or plane and bring it in to show the class.
c. Produce a pamphlet to show the development of either the automobile or the airplane.
d. Estimate the cost of owning an automobile today. Collect necessary information including purchase price and cost of insurance, license plates, gasoline, and maintenance, and present the information in outline form.

Analysis: Determine the changes in American life caused by the automobile and airplane.

Synthesis: Make up a new ad campaign for your favorite auto.

Evaluation: Devise three improvements in automobile and/or airplane safety.

Ideas in Bloom

American Cities

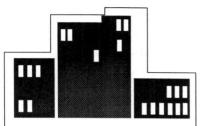

Knowledge: Name five large U.S. cities.

Comprehension: Compare your cities in size and population. Reorganize your list of cities based on population. Determine the location of these cities on a map, and cite their latitudes and longitudes.

Application: Investigate the growth of cities between 1870 and 1900. Collect information and be prepared to discuss your findings with the class.

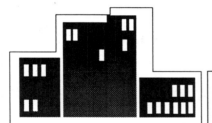

Analysis: Identify problems connected to city life. Survey a group of ten classmates to discover which problem is viewed as the most serious.

Synthesis: Create a collage of pictures and words that reflect the sights and sounds of city life.

Evaluation: Contrast life in the city to life in the country. Decide where you would prefer to live. Support your decision with a minimum of three reasons.

Attractions

Knowledge: Choose five brochures for places to visit. List the names and locations of the attractions described in them.

Comprehension: Read a brochure of your choice. Reword the information given. Use your write-up as you design a poster to advertise the attraction.

Application: Find more information about one of the cities listed. Locate the city on a map and record a minimum of five facts about the city or its attractions.

Analysis: Compare three brochures. What do they have in common? What are their differences?

Synthesis: Arrange the information given to create a whole new look to the advertisement. Design a new cover.

Evaluation: Using your brochures, choose a vacation destination for your family. Justify your decision.

Ideas in Bloom

Name _____   Date _____

Canals, Rivers, and Roads

Knowledge: Label the following on a map of the United States: National Road, Lancaster Turnpike, the Erie Canal, the Pennsylvania Main Line Canal, the Missouri River, the Ohio River, and the Mississippi River.

Comprehension: List the merits and drawbacks of rivers, roads, and canals for transporting agricultural products and manufactured goods.

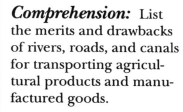

Application: Develop a news story announcing the completion of the Erie Canal. Be as specific with facts as possible.

Analysis: Determine the changes caused by steamboats to the system of transporting goods.

Synthesis: Create your own town. Draw a map showing major roads, waterways, and places of interest. Your town may be from the past, the present, or the future. Be sure to label items and/or make a key. Write a descriptive report to accompany your drawing.

Evaluation: You are a western farmer in the 1800s. Choose a method for transporting your goods to a market in the East. Give reasons for your choice.

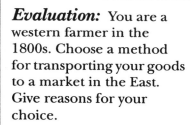

Ideas in Bloom

Careers

Knowledge:

List the fifteen career areas that encompass most careers.

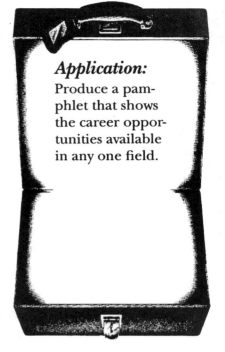

Comprehension:

Generate a list of careers being considered by members of your group. If necessary, poll other groups until your list totals twenty-five or more possible careers. Place each of these careers in the appropriate fifteen career areas.

Application:

Produce a pamphlet that shows the career opportunities available in any one field.

Analysis: Investigate

one career of your choosing to discover the education, skills, and attributes that are desirable for a person pursuing that career.

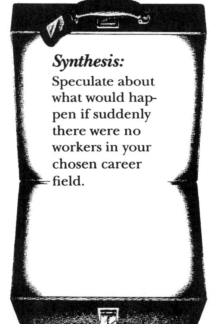

Synthesis:

Speculate about what would happen if suddenly there were no workers in your chosen career field.

Evaluation: Examine the fifteen career areas and decide which will be important in the next century. Rank the areas in order from most important to least important. Justify your choices.

Ideas in Bloom

Computers

Knowledge:
- Diagram and label the computer on which you are working.

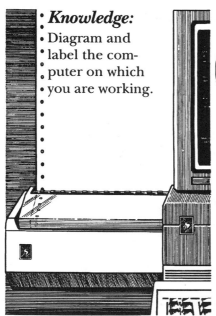

Comprehension:
Explain the following terms relative to computers:

qwerty keyboard
gigo
on-line
options
disk
WYSIWYG
upload/download
justify
program

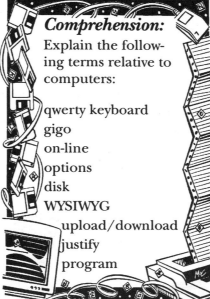

Application:
- Write a script for explaining to a computer novice how to load, run, and shut down a program of your choice.

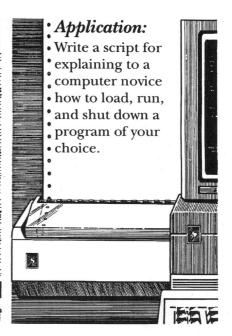

Analysis: On a diagram or poster, depict how the computer is like a typewriter, a tape recorder, a television, a photocopier, a file cabinet, and a musical synthesizer.

Synthesis:
- Choose a career field that interests you and determine how computers are used in that field.
- Prepare a poster or brochure explaining the importance of computer literacy with regard to this career.

Evaluation:
Draw up a set of rules or laws that you think should govern computer use worldwide. Rank in order the top five and tell why you believe them to be crucial.

Ideas in Bloom

The Environment

Knowledge: Collect newspaper articles, magazine articles, and pictures that deal with environmental issues.

Knowledge: Define the following: endangered species, the greenhouse effect, pollution, recycle, ozone layer, fluorocarbon, landfill, smog, biodegradable, and rain forest.

Comprehension: Explain how President Theodore Roosevelt acted as a conservationist while in office.

Comprehension: Choose one of the vocabulary words from the second "Knowledge" activity and illustrate the definition in the form of a cartoon.

Application: Make a collage using the items collected for the first "Knowledge" task.

Analysis: Write an informative speech on local or state environmental concerns and the programs initiated to address them.

Synthesis: Design a poster that encourages people to recycle.

Evaluation: Persuade others that the environment needs to be cared for. Write a letter to the editor of your local paper. Be sure to include your purpose in writing and facts learned from your research and from class discussions.

Ideas in Bloom

Field Trip (Away We Go!)

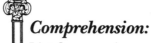

Knowledge: Recall ten facts about the field trip. You may include specific facts about the trip as well as descriptions of time spent with friends.

Comprehension: List five ways in which the trip related to class lessons and discussions.

Application: Organize a field trip for your class. Determine the destination, means of travel, cost, and times of departure, arrival, and return to school. Record all information and be prepared to share with the class.

Analysis: Select three locations in your area that would be desirable for a class field trip. Survey classmates to determine their preferences. Graph your results.

Synthesis: Imagine you are on the tourist board and have the responsibility of increasing the number of visitors to your area. Design a pamphlet or poster that profiles areas of interest in your city or state.

Evaluation: Interpret the graph results (from the analysis task) of another student. Write a brief summary of the results.

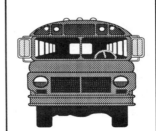

Evaluation: Recommend an area of interest that you would like to explore on a future field trip. Support the recommendation with three to five reasons.

Ideas in Bloom

From Melting Pot to Salad Bowl: Multicultural America

Knowledge: On a map of the United States, locate ten or more ethnic communities. Compare your map with at least three others, making whatever additions or corrections are needed.

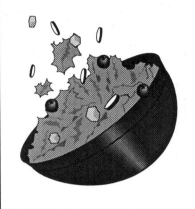

Comprehension: Choose a culture other than your own and report on where the people of that culture settled, why they chose that spot, how they contributed to the unique character of the area, and at least one craft or food they brought with them and popularized.

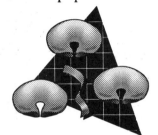

Application: Make a book or video about multiculturalism in your own community, county, or state.

Analysis: A _culture_ can be defined as any group that is joined by common goals, needs, and/ or belief systems. As such, each of us is multicultural, belonging to many cultures at once. Brainstorm a list of elements of typical cultures.

Synthesis: Devise a game that requires players to make choices about tolerance and understanding. Remember to add an element of luck to keep the game challenging.

Evaluation: Decide which five elements of culture are most important and rank them. Give reasons for your choices.

Evaluation: Make a list of ways America is (or was) like a melting pot and another list of ways she is (or was) like a salad bowl. Which do you think is the more nearly accurate image today? Why?

Ideas in Bloom

Handicaps

Knowledge: List the provisions of Public Law 94–142 and the Americans with Disabilities Act.

Comprehension: Brainstorm a list of at least fifteen visible and invisible handicaps that affect schoolchildren.

Application: Choose a handicap to study in depth. Make a data tent to display your findings.

Analysis: Keep a journal of the things you do for one week. Assess how being handicapped would have affected those activities. Rewrite your journal as though you were physically or mentally challenged and wanted to have exactly the same week.

Synthesis: Produce a brochure about your handicap. Make it suitable for placement in the school's guidance office. Be sure to include addresses of national organizations that provide information and of any local support groups you discover.

Evaluation: Rank the handicaps studied by your class, listing them according to which you would find easiest to assume if you were forced to live forever with a handicap. Explain the rationale for at least your first and last choices.

Homelessness

Knowledge: Investigate the estimated number of homeless people in your area and state. Report to the class.

Knowledge: Summarize the 1987 Stewart B. McKinney Homeless Assistance Act.

Comprehension: Chart the effects of homelessness on your area and state.

Application: Illustrate a typical scene involving the homeless.

Analysis: Research Jane Addams's opening of Hull House in Chicago in 1889. How did the problems Addams addressed compare with those that exist today?

Synthesis: Propose a bill that would eliminate most of the educational barriers for homeless children.

Evaluation: List five or more factors that you believe are the key elements of homelessness and rank them in order of importance. Give reasons for your choices.

Maps

Knowledge: Identify the following: political map, road map, graphic-relief map, weather map, chart, topographic map, natural resource map, and globe.

Comprehension: On a map, poster, or mobile, mount or draw an illustration of eight of the following physical features: canyon, gulf, lake, plain, river, strait, valley, peninsula, isthmus, fjord, delta, island, harbor, continent, mountain, and ocean.

Application: Make a detailed map of your school or of your neighborhood.

Analysis: At certain times in history, maps have been considered so important that they were kept secret. List at least eight reasons why a map might be kept secret.

Analysis: Describe the differences and similarities between Mercator's map, Lambert's map, and fixed-point projection maps.

Synthesis: Create and map a fictional continent on which you locate at least twelve different types of physical features. Use at least four features that were not listed in the comprehension activity.

Evaluation: Assess the advantages maps have over globes and vice versa. Give reasons for your answers.

The Newspaper

Knowledge: Name the sections of the newspaper. Describe the types of articles included in each.

Comprehension: Clip out two articles from the newspaper. Rewrite the articles in your own words.

Application: Organize your own newspaper. Be sure to include the sections named in the "Knowledge" task. Begin collecting sample features from the daily paper to include in your project.

Analysis: Select several articles from your collection to include in your paper. Point out the key facts in each.

Synthesis: Publish your paper. Organize your articles so that your paper's format resembles that of a real newspaper. Create your own classified section. In the sports section, include a report about your PE class or a school team. Combine articles from your collection with the articles you create.

Evaluation: Consider the statement, "I don't read the newspaper. Why should I? I can get the same information by watching the evening news." Decide if this is true and explain your reasons.

Political Cartoons

Knowledge: Collect five or more political cartoons.

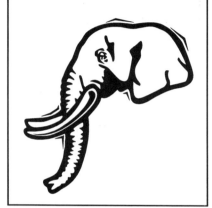

Comprehension: Write a one-paragraph summary of each cartoon. As you explain the cartoonist's message, be sure to allude to the cutline (title) and any other words used in the cartoon, the symbols and illustrations, and any exaggeration used.

Application: Choose an issue about which you have strong feelings—a classroom rule you disagree with or national policy or something in between—and sketch a cartoon to illustrate your position.

Analysis: Find a newspaper story that has been treated both in straight news and in a cartoon. If you can find a related feature story, syndicated column, or editorial on the subject, include it. How do they differ? What facts are exaggerated, omitted, overlooked, or slanted by the cartoonist in an attempt to make a point? Present your findings on a poster.

Analysis: Research an influential political cartoonist such as Thomas Nast, Bill Mauldin, Burt Tolburt, or Milt Morris. Share your findings with the class.

Synthesis: Formulate a set of rules, principles, or standards that you think should govern political cartoons.

Evaluation: Decide which is likely to exert the most influence on the casual newspaper reader—a news story (or series of stories), an editorial, or a political cartoon. Justify your choice.

Ideas in Bloom

Presidents and Their First Ladies

Knowledge: Make a list of United States presidents and their first ladies.

Comprehension: Design a game, puzzle, or maze that requires matching presidents to first ladies or requires knowledge of the sequence of presidential terms of office.

Application: Choose one president and his first lady to study further. Compose a letter the first lady might have written to her husband during his term of office. In the letter, support one of his decisions or give reasons why you disagree with it.

Analysis: Make one list of the attributes you think it is important for a president to have and another list of important attributes of first ladies. Check off the qualities present in the president and first lady you studied.

Synthesis: Speculate how the roles of president and spouse will be altered when America elects a woman president.

Evaluation: Rank the top five presidents and top five first ladies. Disregard whether they were married to one another—you might choose Mary Todd Lincoln without choosing Abraham Lincoln, or vice versa. Give reasons for your choices.

Name _____   Date _____

Sports Heroes

Knowledge: Cluster the following according to the type of sport the person is most noted for: Sonja Henie, Arnold Palmer, Joe DiMaggio, Jim Brown, Jackie Joyner Kersey, Henry Aaron, Ty Cobb, Joe Namath, Bobby Hull, Eddie Arcaro, Lou Gehrig, Bobby Orr, Willie Shoemaker, Willie Mays, Chris Evert, Jack Dempsy, Helen Wills Moody, Jack Nicklaus, Johnny Unitas, Babe Ruth, Muhammad Ali, A. J. Foyt, Wilt Chamberlain, Sugar Ray Robinson, Joe Louis, Ben Hogan, Bronko Nagurski, and George Mikan.

Comprehension: Describe various ways of reorganizing the list of athletes.

Application: Collect newspaper articles, photos of present-day sports figures, and other sports memorabilia. Organize your collection into a "sports yearbook" or prepare a class bulletin board display.

Analysis: Select a person you admire in the sports world. Determine if this athlete is a hero.

Synthesis: Compile a list of qualities that would distinguish a person as a hero or heroine.

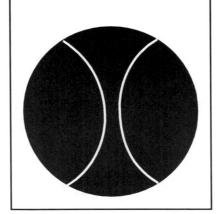

Evaluation: Consider the world of sports. Decide which sport is the best and tell why.

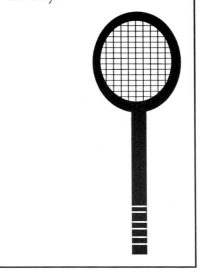

Ideas in Bloom

Television

Knowledge: Summarize the principles on which television operates.

Comprehension: Browse through a weekly TV schedule and make a list of the types of programs listed. Cluster these to form genres.

Application: Design a survey form and survey others about their viewing habits. Compile your results.

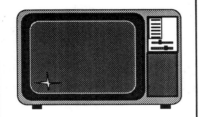

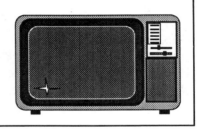

Analysis: Compare a television news story with the newspaper coverage of the same event. Present your conclusions graphically.

Synthesis: Draw conclusions about the concept of law and order in nineteenth-century America and again today by viewing a TV western and a modern police story. Interview a law enforcement officer about the discrepancies between what is seen on TV and what is actually happening on the streets. Decide how that probably applies to the western. Present your findings in an oral report.

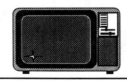

Evaluation: Choose a favorite TV program. Defend its characteristics as representative of or unique to its genre.

There's No Place Like Home

Knowledge: Write a letter to the local tourism board or chamber of commerce requesting information on your area.

Comprehension: Draw a large map of your state or province. Fill in the map with names of cities, towns, waterways, historical sites, and other important features.

Application: Collect information about your state or province. Select events from history, facts about famous people and places, and other newsworthy items. Present this information in the form of a travel brochure or pamphlet.

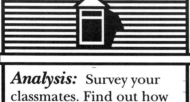

Analysis: Survey your classmates. Find out how many were born in your area, how many moved here from another locale, and how many anticipate moving away within the next five years.

Synthesis: Make up a new name for your state or province. Design a seal and a flag and choose a motto.

Evaluation: Consider the work of fellow classmates. Select the top five designs (from the synthesis task). Rank your choices, the first on the list being the best. Defend your decision.

Ideas in Bloom

Time

Knowledge: List five means or devices by which we measure time.

Comprehension: Illustrate five different time measurement devices.

Application: Trace the development of the calendar and show your findings on a time line or flow chart.

Analysis: Consider what clocks, calendars, sundials, hourglasses, and star charts have in common and how they differ. Find a way to present your conclusions to the class.

Synthesis: Invent a new device for measuring time. Explain its workings to the class.

Evaluation: Determine the consequences if suddenly the world were unable to agree on how to mark the passage of time. Tell which three consequences would be the most sweeping and give your reasons.

Ideas in Bloom

Women in History

Knowledge: Identify the following:

Sojourner Truth
Emma Willard
Harriet Tubman
Elizabeth Gurley Flynn
Frances Perkins
Dorothea Dix
Susan B. Anthony
Elizabeth Cady Stanton
Mary Lyon
Lucretia Coffin
   Mott
Lucy Hobbs Taylor
Jeanette Rankin

Comprehension: Summarize the need for equal rights for men and women.

Application: Predict what life will be like for women in the future.

Analysis: Research one of the women listed in the "Knowledge" task. Write a report detailing her life and accomplishments.

Synthesis: Develop a skit that will demonstrate the changes in the lives of women from the past to the present.

Evaluation: Consider the changes in women's rights since the 1800s. Decide which advancement is the most meaningful to all women. Defend your answer.

Ideas in Bloom

Writers Who Shaped History

Knowledge: Construct a time line on which you place fifteen writers who shaped American history to 1865.

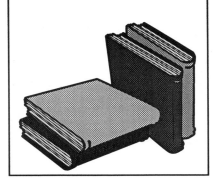

Comprehension: Reorganize your list of writers to show which ones wrote about religious subjects, which wrote about historical or political subjects, and which wrote primarily to entertain. Determine where your time line can be broken generally into these three areas.

Application: Design a poster or use a graphic organizer to illustrate the connections between your writers and the historical events about which they helped to shape thought.

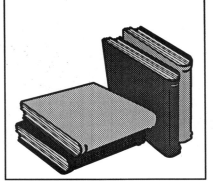

Analysis: Choose one of your writers to research. Analyze how that writer's works influenced history and present your findings to the class.

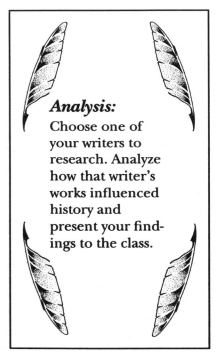

Synthesis: Compose a poem or story about a current social problem. Be sure to suggest at least one solution.

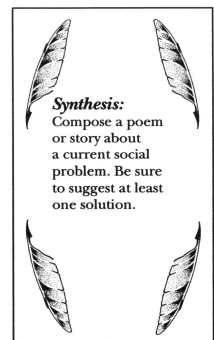

Evaluation: Decide which is most important in changing history: religion, politics, or literature. Justify your choice.

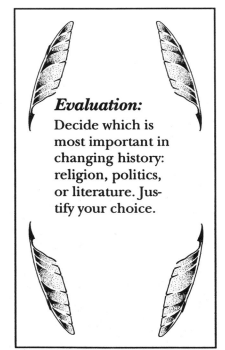

Ideas in Bloom

WATERING THE BLOOMS: TEACHER NOTES AND ANSWERS FOR ACTIVITY PAGES

This section of the book presented the sharpest challenge for the writers for several reasons. One was the issue of voice: though we have tried to avoid arbitrary and autocratic responses, the written sources we studied often presented so little diversity that there seemed to be little room for other answers. If there are places where you disagree with our presentation, your voice should be the one your students hear. For the most part, we have attempted to provide sample or representative answers anywhere there is room for disagreement.

Another challenge was the issue of complexity. We did not want to insult colleagues by providing answers that were elementary, but at the same time, we recognize that often teachers are assigned teaching opportunities for which they have little or no background and that long-term substitutes are asked to teach subjects that are not their area of expertise; these are the teachers most likely to seek out supplementary teaching materials like these. So we strove for balance, knowing that the more experienced, knowledgeable teacher will cast a cursory glance at the answer pages, but that other teachers will appreciate not having to consult numerous other sources in order to use the activity pages.

We decided, too, that we wanted to separate straight answers from thinking process models: thus, the "Pump Primers" were born. Identifying material as a Pump Primer is little different from a newspaper's telling readers that an article on the front page is commentary, rather than straight news: it is a disclaimer. Pump Primers are designed to get students thinking and theorizing; they do not have specific answers. They can be used or ignored without significantly affecting factual content.

Our use of words like "discuss," "explain," "share," or "demonstrate" is deliberately vague. These terms could refer to written or oral products, and it's up the the teacher to decide which is preferable. If class time and teacher preference tend toward oral activities, "oral skills" can be added as an area of purpose.

Pre-Columbian America

Purpose

As a result of completing the activities on this Bloom sheet, the students will demonstrate growth in the following areas:

1. explaining how and why people move themselves across the earth;

2. perceiving the dynamic relationship between geography and history;

3. demonstrating a knowledge of place and location by creating a map;

4. organizing information in a rubric; and

5. identifying likenesses and differences in dissimilar data.

Knowledge: [Tell how the first people might have come to America and what their lives were probably like after they arrived.] While most students will allude to the Siberians crossing the Bering land bridge during the last ice age, there are numerous other theories that cannot be discounted out of hand: Some people believe the first Americans came by boat from China, Japan, or Polynesia. Others believe they were descendants of the Ten Lost Tribes of Israel. Still others believe they were descended from early Europeans whose boats were blown off course by storms or trade winds. There's even a theory that they were able to cross the Atlantic via the so-called "lost continent of Atlantis."

Comprehension: [Map the Bering land bridge and the possible migration routes through North America.] Maps will be inexact because we have no way of knowing the size or shape of the glaciers; however, it is important that there be a sizable ice bridge across the Bering Strait. Students should understand that migration routes typically followed the edges of mountain ranges and the courses of rivers. Any cartographers who indicate probable migration routes on their maps have commonly back-formed these routes from the known areas of settlement.

Application: [Think as an anthropologist does. Write a paper in which you tell how Native American societies were changed by the coming of the Europeans.] Some considerations are biological consequences, military consequences, and cultural gains. Biological consequences include the introduction of diseases and the effects of intermarriage. Military consequences include the uprooting and exiling of large groups of people; the destruction and looting of cities, burial sites, and religious centers; and the overthrow of governments. Cultural gains might include new crops and livestock and new technologies.

PUMP PRIMER

Student interest in archaeology might be capitalized on here by suggesting a brief biographical study of an anthropologist such as Margaret Mead or Louis Leakey.

Analysis: [Identify and explain major differences among the seven American Indian culture groups. Present your findings in a rubric.] The seven cultures were these: Northwest Coast, California, Great Basin and Plateau, Southwest, Great Plains, Eastern Woodlands, and Southeast. Cultural aspects students may need to consider are major tribes, terrain and environment, food sources, housing, and tools, weapons, and utensils. Students may not be familiar with the term "rubric." Only newer references will adequately define it. As used here, it names any decorative grid or chart that organizes data graphically.

Synthesis: [Imagine that you belonged to one of the culture groups in pre-Columbian America. Construct a folktale or legend that reveals part of the history and the values of your culture.] Writings will vary.

Evaluation: [Decide which of the seven cultures you would have preferred to live in. Give reasons for your choice.] Answers will vary.

Christopher Columbus

Purpose

As a result of completing the activities on this Bloom sheet, the students will demonstrate growth in the following areas:

1. identifying and applying appropriate time concepts;

2. explaining the impact of an individual on historical development;

3. utilizing appropriate geographical reference, study, and critical thinking skills to make decisions and solve a problem;

4. relating economic and political conditions to historical change; and

5. identifying the appropriate source to obtain information using print materials and technology.

Knowledge: [List three facts about Christopher Columbus.] Facts about Columbus include the following: he was born in Genoa, Italy, in 1451. He loved the sea. He moved to Lisbon, Portugal, in 1476. By 1484, Columbus had decided to seek a western route to the East Indies. His first wife, Felipa, died. He had two sons, Diego and Ferdinand. He sought financing from King Ferdinand and Queen Isabella of Spain. The three ships included in the expedition were the *Niña*, the *Pinta*, and the *Santa María*. Columbus made several voyages to the new world. He died in 1506.

Comprehension: [Relate the story of Christopher Columbus's discovery of America in the form of a skit.] Responses will vary. In the interests of time and order, you may want to put students into small groups to complete this task.

Application: [On chart paper, show the sequence of events leading to Columbus's discovery.] Responses will vary.

Analysis: [Research the life of Christopher Columbus and write a two-page report.] Responses will vary.

PUMP PRIMER ———

Less able students may treat this as a knowledge task by consulting only one source. More capable students should pull data from more than one source and consolidate it.

Analysis: [Speculate on what Columbus might have done if Queen Isabella had not financed his trip.] Responses will vary.

PUMP PRIMER ———

Although students relate easily to the role of Isabella as a world leader, her role was certainly not typical for a woman in her culture. Students might want to explore the rights and roles of women in the Spanish culture of Columbus's time.

Synthesis: [Plan a trip to the Bahamas. What would you need to take with you if you were traveling by boat? Compare your trip to the trip Columbus made.] Responses will vary. You may wish to provide a structure within which students are to operate.

One effective problem-solving strategy is the following:

define the problem

list alternatives

list probable consequences for each alternative

establish criteria

evaluate alternatives, measuring them against the criteria established and the consequences listed

make a decision

Evaluation: [Compare Columbus's financing of his trip with the financial tactics of modern explorers. Decide which is the most feasible method and give reasons for your choice.] Students may need to research some modern explorers and the methods of financing they employ. Suggestions for starting their investigation include looking at the Antarctic explorers who found backing in the business world; at treasure hunters, who often form limited partnerships that combine business backing with reinvestment of part of the profits from previous sunken ship recoveries; at medical researchers, whose work is often financed by drug companies, universities, private and public grants, and tax dollars; and at space explorers, who are financed almost exclusively by taxation. Students could also be given a list of specific explorers to investigate, for example, Solomon Andreas, Jacques Cousteau, Amelia Earhart, and John Glenn.

ADDITIONAL TEACHER RESOURCES

Pirates, Explorers, Trailblazers. Learning Works Enrich-

ment Series. Santa Barbara, Calif.: The Learning Works, Inc., 1987.

Levinson, Nancy Smiler. *Christopher Columbus: Voyager to the Unknown.* New York: Lodestar Books, 1990. Chronology at 106–107.

———

Early Explorers

Purpose

As a result of completing the activities on this Bloom sheet, the students will demonstrate growth in the following areas:

1. applying a problem-solving technique or process;

2. consolidating information from many sources into a new product;

3. oral skills;

4. explaining the impact of individuals, trends, and events on historical development; and

5. relating economic and political conditions to historical change.

Knowledge: [Select three of the explorers listed below. Tell of their discoveries in North America.]

John Cabot discovered the North American continent.

Giovanni da Verrazano was the first man to explore the coastal area from North Carolina to Newfoundland and write an account of his experiences.

Jacques Cartier discovered the St. Lawrence River and the Gulf of St. Lawrence.

Martin Frobisher rounded the tip of Greenland and discovered a large body of water now known as Frobisher Bay.

Samuel de Champlain explored the St. Lawrence area and the Great Lakes and founded the city of Quebec.

Henry Hudson explored the Chesapeake Bay area.

Lewis Joliet explored what is now known as the Mississippi River.

Robert Cavelier, Sieur de La Salle claimed all the land drained by the Mississippi for France.

Comprehension: [Suggest reasons why there was a keen desire to find a northwest passage.] Students should realize that Europeans were eager to trade with Asia. They were still unaware of the riches to be found in the North American continent.

Application: [Prepare a list of supplies needed for an expedition into the "unknown" territories of the North American continent.] This application activity could be done as a cooperative learning activity such as the circle of knowledge.

The circle of knowledge is a brainstorming technique that works best when participants are divided into groups of four to six participants and group members are seated in a circle. One person in each group is designated as the recorder and all other participants take turns supplying a response to the same stimulus/question for a specific number of rounds or until time

is called. If you choose, you may allow participants to pass once; otherwise, every participant (except the recorder) should answer in turn each time. When time is called, another minute or two should be designated as time for the recorder to make additions.

This procedure has several advantages over typical brainstorming exercises. Because students are in a small group setting, it is easier to keep more vocal students from dominating the session and to keep quiet students from fading into the background. The process is orderly and involves every child.

Once each group has its list, a master list can be compiled by repeating the process, allowing each recorder to respond in turn around the room.

Analysis: [Suppose an efficient route to Asia from Europe had existed. What effect would that have had on the settling of the North American continent?] Answers will vary.

Synthesis: [Write a three-act play depicting the life and times of one of the explorers. Perform your original play for the class.] You may want to divide the class into four groups. Have each group create a play to dramatize the life of one of the explorers. Students should work cooperatively to write their own dialogue, trying to recreate the sights, sounds, and drama of the times in which these men lived. Tasks assigned to group members might include the actual script writing, set design, costumes, and props. Performers should be from the group. All group

members need to participate equally.

Evaluation: [Decide which group did the best in the following categories: script, costumes, overall performance, most historically realistic. Award the group a Certificate of Appreciation.] Answers will vary. Students should devise a score sheet that lists the evaluative criteria they will use. Avoid a popularity contest.

You may award a commercially prepared certificate; however, an additional synthesis activity can be created by having students design the certificates to be used.

The Salem Witchcraft Trials

Purpose

As a result of completing the activities in this unit, the students will demonstrate growth in the following areas:

1. explaining the effects of a major belief system on historical development;

2. applying a problem-solving technique or process;

3. perceiving events and issues as they were experienced by people at that time to develop historic empathy as opposed to present-mindedness;

4. identifying similarities and differences between modern society and a historic culture; and

5. oral skills.

Knowledge: [Retell the story of the Salem Witchcraft Trials.] Although the answers will vary, mention should be made of Anne Hutchinson and Tituba and of the end result: 19 women and 2 dogs were hanged, 1 man was pressed to death, and 31 people were convicted of witchcraft. All told, over 140 were accused, more than 100 of them women.

Comprehension: [Explain the cultural belief system that enabled the witchcraft accusations to be taken seriously.] Important to an understanding of the culture are these ideas:

Religious freedom was defined as being able to worship in the Puritan way, without question.

The church was seen as having absolute authority directly mandated by God.

Women were expected to be silent, obedient, and unquestioning.

Slaves from the West Indies and other places had brought with them their folk tales of Obeah (voodoo), sorcery, and witchcraft.

It was widely accepted that children were incapable of lying.

Unexplained healing and folk medicines were believed to come from Satan.

Application: [Pose a series of questions that might be used by a court of inquiry investigating the witchcraft accusations.] Answers will vary.

PUMP PRIMER ————————

Decide in advance whether you also want students to construct answers to their own questions or whether you wish to use the questions as discussion starters.

One activity students might enjoy would be to play "Pass the Problem," a cooperative learning strategy. Select a number of questions to be used: for discussion purposes let's assume six. Write each question on the outside of an envelope. Divide students into six groups (equal to the number of questions) and give each group six slips of paper and one of the prepared envelopes.

Each group then discusses its question and decides on an answer that fits the facts. Writing from the prescribed point of view (for instance, the Salem Puritans'), the recorder records the group's answer on one slip of paper and encloses the paper in the envelope. When time is called, each group passes its problem to the next group. Groups should not look at previous answers.

The process is repeated until every group has responded to every question. Envelopes are then collected by the teacher or moderator and answers are read. As each question is answered, you may want to allow for "minority opinions" to be expressed, for comments on other groups' answers, and for other discussion. Students may choose to vote on or reach consensus on a "best" answer, or may agree to disagree.

Analysis: [Discover the reasons why Anne Hutchinson was accused of sorcery. Analyze the extent to which those same prejudices exist in modern society.] Anne Hutchinson had the effrontery to assume a leadership role and to question the established religion. Such behavior would have been merely scandalous in a man, but was heresy coming from a woman. Hutchinson was excommunicated from the church and banished from the town. Later (1643) she was murdered by Indians. Students' assessments of lingering prejudice will vary.

Synthesis: [Rewrite your answer to the knowledge activity in a contemporary setting, making whatever changes might be necessary.] Responses will vary. If students have difficulty starting this assignment, you may wish to brainstorm some scenarios or to find news stories of people falsely accused of crimes, improper sexual behavior, or other aberrant behavior.

Evaluation: [Determine the consequences in today's society of leveling false accusations. Give as many examples as you can think of. Decide which set of consequences is harsher, those in today's society or those in Salem. Defend your answer.] Encourage students to think of the effects on both the accused and the accuser. Have them consider not only legal consequences, but also of hidden, civil consequences. Rumor and innuendo, for example, could cost a person a marriage or a career without anyone's waiting for a trial. Decide in advance how you want this information presented.

CONNECTING TO LITERATURE

Students might enjoy reading Elizabeth George Speare's *The Witch of Blackbird Pond* and Arthur Miller's *The Crucible.*

The French and Indian War

Purpose

As a result of completing the activities on this Bloom sheet, students will demonstrate growth in the following areas:

1. explaining the impact of individuals, events, and trends on historical and economic development;

2. recognizing that there are multiple possible interpretations of any historical event;

3. explaining how contemporary and future civilizations have been influenced by past events;

4. speculating on differences that might have resulted had another point of view prevailed;

5. relating economic and political conditions to historical change; and

6. perceiving events and issues as they were experienced by people at that time to develop historical empathy as opposed to present-mindedness.

Knowledge: [Prepare a bulletin board about the French and Indian War.] Products will vary.

Comprehension: [Write a letter to Prime Minister Pitt presenting the colonists' views on recruitment, confiscation, and quarter-ing.] Responses will vary but should be consistent with these ideas: most colonists opposed forced conscription, confiscation of supplies, and forced housing of troops in private homes. You may wish to guide students in a discussion of the different belief systems of the patriots and the loyalists.

Application: [Pretend you are one of the following: General Edward Braddock, General James Wolfe, or General Louis Montcalm. Write a diary entry for a day significant to the French and Indian War.] Responses will vary.

Analysis: [Explain how and why the colonists prospered during (and because of) the war.] Considerations will include increased trade (colonists sold crops and goods to both armies), increased military experience, increased business for the ship-building industry, and opportunities for westward expansion. Decide in advance whether you want this to be a written or oral activity.

Synthesis: [Speculate about how different life would be today if the Treaty of Paris had left control of Canada and the Louisiana Territory with the French instead of giving it to Britain. Write a narrative or draw a picture to show some of the significant differences.] Responses will vary.

Evaluation: [Examine the French and Indian War from the Native American point of view. Both the French and the English had Indian allies. With which side would you have aligned yourself? Give reasons.] Answers will vary.

The American Revolution

Purpose

As a result of completing the activities on this Bloom sheet, the students will demonstrate growth in the following areas:

1. citing reasons for the American Revolution;

2. explaining the importance of the Battle of Saratoga;

3. demonstrating a knowledge of place and location by creating a map; and

4. relating economic and political conditions to historical change.

Knowledge: [Identify the following:]

Prime Minister George Grenville had become prime minister of Great Britain after the French and Indian War. Grenville was responsible for enforcing the Navigation Acts and the Stamp Act.

Paul Revere, a silversmith by trade, was a member of the Sons of Liberty. He was instrumental in warning citizens that the British were marching out of Boston. Paul Revere's home is open to tourists, and is located on Boston's Freedom Trail.

Crispus Attucks was one of the more than 5,000 African Americans who served on the patriot side in the American Revolution.

Attucks was the first victim—and perhaps the first martyr—of the Revolution. An escaped slave, Attucks was one of five men shot at the so-called Boston Massacre on March 5, 1770. A Boston artist recorded the massacre in a drawing that was copied and circulated by Paul Revere. Jefferson was later to comment that Attucks's blood "nourished the tree of liberty."

The Stamp Act was a law requiring the colonists to fix a tax stamp to newspapers, letters, wills, deeds, and other papers. The cost of the stamps varied from a few cents to a few dollars.

The Navigation Acts provided that the colonists were to sell certain products only to Great Britain or to the other colonies. Products were to be sent to Britain for taxation and were required to be transported by British ships.

The Proclamation of 1763 was ordered to prevent further settlement west of the Appalachians.

PUMP PRIMER

Many legal papers today, including deeds, chattel loans, and mortgages, require the purchase and affixing of documentary (doc) stamps. Students might be interested in investigating the similarity between doc stamps and the tax stamps being required by Great Britain. Discussion might lead to speculation about why the one is acceptable and the other was not.

The doc stamp is just one of many excise taxes. What other taxes can students discover? Perhaps this would be a good time to invite a tax expert to talk

to the class about visible and invisible taxes.

PUMP PRIMER

Students who wish to learn more about the contribution of African Americans to the war effort might enjoy reading Burke Davis's *Black Heroes of the American Revolution* (HBJ, 1976). Though the book has fewer than eighty pages of text, it is chock full of information about a people often neglected in what the author refers to as "white history books."

Students might also be encouraged to investigate the role of Native Americans in this war, especially the Creek Indians, who largely aided the British, and the Cherokee, who fought on the patriot side.

Comprehension: [Explain the slogan No Taxation without Representation.] The colonists felt that since they did not elect anyone to Parliament, Parliament had no right to tax them.

Application: [Prepare a colorful map of the Saratoga Campaign. Be sure to include a title and a legend.] Most textbooks or encyclopedias will provide a model for students to use in preparing their maps. If you prefer, you could duplicate an outline map for them to use as a starting point.

Analysis: [Point out three cultural differences between Britain and America that significantly affected the war.] Answers will vary but might include the following:

- There were more people living in Great Britain than in America.

- America had a small army and no navy.

- There were only a few factories in America.

- There was a very well organized government in Great Britain.

Synthesis: [Suppose that Parliament had repealed the Tea Tax and the Intolerable Acts and that war had not broken out. How would life be different if there had been no American Revolution?] Answers will vary.

Evaluation: [Defend the idea that the Battle of Saratoga was the turning point of the war.] After the Battle of Saratoga, France viewed America as being capable of defeating Great Britain. America would gain greatly by being recognized by France.

CONNECTING TO LITERATURE

This is a good place to study Longfellow's poem "The Midnight Ride of Paul Revere." Students might be interested in investigating the historical inaccuracies in the poem. They may also want to know that Revere was only one of several riders, but his fame obscures theirs, largely because of this poem.

Students might also enjoy reading Iris Van Rynback's *The Soup Stone* (Greenwillow, 1988). Discuss the reasons why this version might have been set in post-Revolutionary America, rather than in Sweden or France, as earlier versions were. Why is the stone soup cooked up for soldiers, rather than for a hobo, as in some versions? How does it reflect cultural values?

ADDITIONAL STUDENT READINGS

Avi, *The Fighting Ground*

Patricia Clapp, *I'm Deborah Sampson: A Soldier in the War of the Revolution*

Patricia Edwards Clyne, *Patriots in Petticoats*

James and Christopher Collier, *Blood Country*

_____ , *My Brother Sam Is Dead*

Esther Forbes, *Johnny Tremain*

Freedom's Documents

Purpose

As a result of completing the activities on this Bloom sheet, the students will demonstrate growth in the following areas:

1. organizing information in an expository article format;

2. identifying fundamental beliefs inherent in the Declaration of Independence and the U.S. Constitution;

3. using a graphic organizer to summarize information; and

4. speculating on differences that might have resulted from another point of view.

Knowledge: [Write a one-paragraph summary of the provisions of the Articles of Confederation, the Constitution, the Declaration of Independence, and the Bill of Rights.]

The Articles of Confederation. Drafted in York, Pennsylvania, in 1777, this document formed a loose alignment of the thirteen colonies and listed the powers of government and the powers of states. The government was given control of all western land holdings. Major provisions include one state, one vote, requiring nine votes to pass legislation; power to borrow money, wage war, and make peace; and power to settle boundary disputes, trade with Indians, and provide mail service, but no power to create a central judiciary, to regulate trade, to tax, or to issue money.

The Constitution. Meeting at Independence Hall in Philadelphia in 1787, fifty-five delegates from twelve states drafted a new constitution to replace the Articles of Confederation. The Constitution established a bicameral legislature, three branches of government, a system of checks and balances, issues of presidency, and limitations on slave trade. It also gave the government the authority to regulate trade, levy taxes, and coin money.

The Declaration of Independence. A congressional order written in 1776, this document declared that the colonies were free and independent states. Signed in Philadelphia on July 4, the Declaration gave a rationale for writing the document, outlined the purposes of government, listed charges against the king, described attempts to obtain justice, and declared independence.

The Bill of Rights. Suggested by the Federalists to appease John Adams and the Massachusetts convention, the Bill of Rights is the title given collectively to the first ten amendments to the Constitution. These amendments established basic rights and freedoms: freedom of religion, speech, press, assembly, and petition; the right to bear arms; limits on quartering; protections against search and seizure; the rights of individuals in courts of law; and a disclaimer of government rights in all unspecified areas.

Comprehension: [Divide chart paper into three columns. In the outer columns, list the views of the opposing sides at the Constitutional Convention. In the center, list the compromises.] Make sure students cover all three proposals: the Great Compromise, the Three-Fifths Compromise, and the Slave Trade Agreement. Answers might look something like this:

Virginia Plan
Each state would be represented according to population
The Great Compromise
two houses, one with two representatives per state and the other with representation based on population with a minimum of one
New Jersey Plan
one state, one vote

North
count slaves in population for taxation, as direct taxation was divided among the states according to population
Three-Fifths Compromise
three of every five slaves were counted for both issues
South
count slaves for representation but not for taxes

North
anti-slavery faction wanted to halt trade
Slave Trade Agreement
put a twenty-year limit on trade before the Congress could again consider the issue
South
slave states refused all limitations

Application: [Create a constitution for your class, club, or school. Include a preamble.] Questions to answer include, How will the group function? How many leaders will there be? How will they be chosen? What characteristics should they have? Who will make up the membership/citizenship? How will you decide who will join? What will happen when citizens/members disagree with government/leadership? To extend the study, have the students design a flag and a symbol.

Analysis: [Make a list of ways life might be different if the United States were still governed by the Articles of Confederation.] Areas to consider include law, money, trade, defense, legislation, international affairs, and so on.

Synthesis: [Interview a signer of the Constitution. Find out what determined his state's decision to ratify. Turn your interview into a newspaper or magazine article.] For most choices, students may want merely to speculate on reasons, but some facts should be included. Rhode Island and North Carolina were persuaded only after the new government was established and it became evident they could not maintain independence. Massachusetts, Virginia, and New York agreed only after extracting a promise of a bill of rights.

Evaluation: [Tell which amendment has the most sweeping effect on your life. Explain your reasoning.] Answers will vary.

The Louisiana Purchase

Purpose

As a result of completing the activities on this Bloom sheet, the students will demonstrate growth in the following areas:

1. explaining the impact of individuals, events, and trends on historical development;

2. interpreting changes made by individuals and events and how these changes can be watershed events;

3. demonstrating a knowledge of place and location by creating a map;

4. consolidating information from many sources into a new product; and

5. identifying the appropriate source to obtain information using print materials and technology.

Knowledge: [Write the answers to the WH questions (who, what, when, where, why, and how) with regard to the Louisiana Purchase.]

Who:	Thomas Jefferson
What:	Louisiana Purchase
Where:	west of the Mississippi River
When:	1803
Why:	to increase size of the United States in order to fulfill our Manifest Destiny and to improve commerce
How:	James Monroe and Robert Livingston were sent to Paris to negotiate the sale. The purchase price was $15 million.

Knowledge: [Search for information about Lewis and Clark. Write down five facts about what they accomplished.] Answers will vary but may include some of these facts:

1. Meriwether Lewis was secretary to Thomas Jefferson.

2. Jefferson asked Lewis to explore the Missouri River.

3. Lewis was instructed to collect data on the plants and animals of the region.

4. William Clark was second in command.

5. They left St. Louis in May 1804.

6. Sacajawea served as a guide for the expedition.

PUMP PRIMER

Sacajawea's role in the Lewis and Clark expedition is often underplayed or even ignored in traditional history texts. Students might enjoy learning more about this courageous native American woman.

Comprehension: [Expand your information from the two "Knowledge" activities into a news article or a TV bulletin informing the American people about the Louisiana Purchase.] Answers will vary.

Application: [Prepare a map of the United States that shows the 530 million-acre area known as the Louisiana Territory. Show the route of Lewis and Clark. Label the Ohio, Mississippi, and Missouri rivers.] Work will vary. Textbooks and encyclopedias should be available for student use and for verifying correctness of responses.

Analysis: [Determine the changes in United States history caused by the purchase of the Louisiana Territory.] Answers may include the following: The United States doubled in size.

The United States was ranked as a world leader. Not only did the U.S. gain control of the Mississippi River, she also gained control of the port of New Orleans. The nation managed to avoid war with France. Other answers are possible.

Synthesis: [Design a character to serve as a mascot for the Lewis and Clark Expedition.] Work will vary. A contest could be held to reward the students for their creativity. For an alternate evaluation activity, students could vote on their favorite mascot.

Evaluation: [Explain your vote for Thomas Jefferson in the presidential election of 1804.] Answers will vary.

PUMP PRIMER

Students need to be aware that Jefferson received 162 electoral votes to Charles Cotesworth Pinckney's 14. Many citizens were pleased that Jefferson was able to keep America at peace and that the western boundaries of the United States had expanded.

California Missions

Purpose

As a result of completing the activities on this Bloom sheet, the students will demonstrate growth in the following areas:

1. articulating the influence of the Spanish on American culture;

2. organizing information in a poster format;

3. explaining the effects of a major belief system on historical patterns of development; and

4. explaining the impact of an individual on historical development.

Knowledge: [Outline information about Father Junipero Serra.] Father Junipero Serra founded the first mission in California in 1769. Father Serra was responsible for opening twenty-one missions along the west coast of California.

Comprehension: [Give examples of Spanish influence that still exist in our society today.] There are numerous examples of Spain's influence here in the United States. The American dollar was modeled after the Spanish peso. Spaniards introduced horses and mules, which greatly affected our way of life. Lemon, orange, and grapefruit trees and other plants were introduced. The Spanish-Mexican style of ranching is apparent, especially in the West. Spanish missionaries helped to spread Christianity. The missions served as models for the present-day reservations. Spanish words are very much a part of our vocabulary. Architectural styles also display a Spanish influence.

PUMP PRIMER

Have students create a collage of pictures and words, instead of a written response. In some communities, it may be appropriate to encourage students who are interested in photography to do a photo essay or montage instead.

Application: [Find ways in which the missionaries positively affected the lives of Native Americans prior to 1800.] Missionaries were sent to convert Native Americans to Christianity. The missions were established to educate the Indians in the Spanish way of life and in skills such as weaving. They were also shown how to farm and how to make dairy products. The missionaries served as a liaison between the Indians and the settlers.

Analysis: [Look into changes made to the missions by the Mexican government between 1834 and 1846.] Spanish rule ended in colonial America in 1822. In 1834, the Mexican Republic decided to return the mission lands to its citizens. The best land was not given to the Indians, however. Instead, the Mexican Republic divided the mission land and set up large estates (*rancheros*). Mission buildings were abandoned, and the Indians became servants to the wealthy landowners.

Synthesis: [Design a poster as an advertisement for a book about Father Junipero Serra.] Products will vary. Students will need to include information from the knowledge task in their answers.

Evaluation: [Decide whether Native Americans were treated fairly by the missionaries and by Spanish law. Justify your response.] Answers will vary. Point out to students that even though Spanish law ostensibly protected Native Americans, Spain was a long distance away from the New World, and the laws were ignored. The mission-

aries themselves forced the Indians to work long hours on the farms. Illness and death often occurred as a result of the introduction of European diseases.

EXTENDING THE STUDY

Students might wish to look into the concept of "sanctuary" the important role it played in the missions of the West. The students might also try to establish how the concept of sanctuary has evolved in American history and to compare government reactions to the concept as it is applied in this country and in other countries.

The Trail of Tears

Purpose

As a result of completing the activities on this Bloom sheet, the students will demonstrate growth in the following areas:

1. demonstrating a knowledge of place and location by creating a map;

2. explaining how a location's significance changes as cultures alter their interactions with each other;

3. identifying the consequences of human alterations of physical environments, both positive and negative;

4. recognizing that there are multiple possible interpretations of historical events;

5. interpreting patterns of behavior that reflected values and attitudes that

posed problems to cross-cultural understanding; and

6. evaluating the degree to which public policy and citizen behaviors realize the stated ideals of a democratic republican form of government.

Knowledge: [Identify each of the following in terms of the practice of Indian removal:]

Manifest Destiny. Manifest Destiny was the philosophical belief that the United States had a God-given right to expand to the Pacific Ocean, regardless of obstacles. Not surprisingly, this issue was debated much more intensely once gold was discovered on Indian lands in 1820.

Andrew Jackson. Elected president in 1829, Jackson was looked up to by many Native Americans who were hopeful that he would be fair to them, as he had promised in his inaugural address. After all, Jackson's life was intertwined with theirs: Cherokee Chief Major (John) Ross had helped Jackson defeat the marauding Creeks; another Cherokee, Junaluska, had saved Jackson's life at the Battle of Horseshoe Bend during the Creek War of 1814. It was, however, Jackson who proposed the Indian Removal Act.

Wendell Phillips. An abolitionist who championed the Indian cause, Phillips was one of a long line of defenders of the Cherokee cause, including Noah Webster, John Adams, Sam Houston, and Davy Crockett.

Martin Van Buren. Jackson's successor's election sealed the Cherokees' fate in Georgia. Van

Buren was described by Davy Crockett as one who could "strut and swagger like a crow in the gutter." Van Buren empowered Scott to remove the Cherokee by force.

Henry B. Whipple.   Whipple was the first Protestant Episcopal bishop of Minnesota. He called for Americans to unite in an effort to see that the Indians were treated fairly.

General Winfield Scott.   Scott led 7,000 soldiers into Georgia to expel the Cherokee forcibly and to transport them to The Indian Territory in what is now Oklahoma.

James M. Cavanaugh. Cavanaugh was the Montana Territory's delegate to Congress whose opposition to Indian causes is well documented. "The only good Indian is a dead Indian" is a familiar paraphrase of a quote attributed to him.

Indian Removal Act.   This act authorized the removal of the southeastern tribes and other Native Americans from their lands in exchange for territory west of the Mississippi River. The act further provided funds and troops to move the 50,000 to 60,000 Indians involved.

Sequoyah.   Also known as George Gist or George Guess, Sequoyah developed the first Indian alphabet, a syllabary of eighty-five characters that represented the Cherokee language and enabled the Cherokee by 1822 to read and write in their own language, the first Indians to do so (and this at a time when many whites were still illiterate).

Treaty of Tellico.   This 1798 treaty with thirty-nine Cherokee leaders guaranteed that the remaining 43,000 square miles of tribal land in Georgia, Alabama, and Mississippi would belong to the Cherokee "forever."

Comprehension: [Map the five civilized tribes and show their routes to The Indian Territory.] The Cherokee, occupying land predominantly in Alabama, Georgia, Tennessee, and the Carolinas, were marched northwest toward what is now Nashville, through western Kentucky, across the Ohio River, through southern Illinois, across the Missouri, and on west and southwest to Oklahoma. Nearly 4,000 died from disease and from lack of food and clothing to protect them from the harsh winter.

The Creek, who had settled along the western bank of the Chattahoochee in Alabama and in part of Georgia, were split into two bands. One group traveled north and west to Memphis, where they were taken by boat down the Mississippi to its junction with the Arkansas and up the Arkansas into The Indian Territory. The other group was forced south to Mobile and New Orleans, up the Mississippi and the Arkansas Rivers to The Territory. Prior to their removal, the Creek had surrendered twenty-three million acres of land in Alabama (approximately half the state, including four million acres that were really Cherokee property) in a peace treaty signed in August 1814.

The Seminoles occupied most of central Florida from the Okeechobee north. They were transported by boat from Tampa Bay to New Orleans, where they followed the rivers to Oklahoma.

The Chocktaw had lived in central Mississippi and part of western Alabama before being forced across the Mississippi near Natchez and overland through Louisiana and Arkansas and into The Territory.

The Chickasaw had settled throughout Mississippi and in parts of Alabama and Tennessee. They crossed the Mississippi at Memphis and traveled in a westerly line across Arkansas to The Territory.

Pump Primer ——————

Besides the five civilized tribes, Indian removal included the Sauk and Fox tribes of Wisconsin and Michigan's upper peninsula, the Ojibway and Ottawa of Wisconsin and Illinois, the Potawatomi and Miami from Indiana, and Ohio's Shawnee. More advanced students might be encouraged to add these tribal routes to their maps.

Application: [Before native Americans had a written language, their history was passed on in oral sagas and hieroglyphic wampum belts. Discover three or more native tales and list some of the things that were important to Native Americans as revealed in their folklore.] Answers will vary. Common threads running through most of the Cherokee tales include these:

- reverence for nature
- animate, humanized nature
- tribal independence
- family closeness
- acceptance of responsibility

- agricultural and industrial occupations
- propensity for war
- honor—a man's word was inviolate and liars were not tolerated
- the good of the tribe comes before the good of self

One good source for Cherokee folklore is *Aunt Mary, Tell Me a Story* by Mary Ulmer Chiltoskey. This book is available from Cherokee Communications, P.O. Box 507, Cherokee, North Carolina 28719. In it, the author cites another source, James Mooney's *Myths of the Cherokee and Sacred Formulas of the Cherokees,* reprinted by Charles and Randy Elder in 1982.

Analysis: [List things the Cherokee did to try to hold on to their tribal lands. Theorize why these actions were unsuccessful. Present your findings in a written format.] Answers will vary, but should include the acceptance and use of the English language, the adopting of English customs, and trade with the English. Also, each of the more than twenty treaties executed between the U.S. and the Cherokee had the Indians forfeiting more of their land in exchange for being given the remaining lands with their "inviolable" boundaries "forever." Additionally, the Cherokee consistently honored their treaties by siding with the English in the War of 1812 and the Creek War of 1814. The Cherokee also fought in the Civil War, although most (including Brig. Gen. Stand Watie) fought for the Confederacy. The Cherokee lost 7,000 men during the Civil War.

PUMP PRIMER

This is a logical place to teach the cultural phenomenon of assimilation. Have students speculate on why Native American assimilation was less successful than the assimilation of groups of white immigrants. More advanced students might try writing an editorial or an essay that attempts to view the assimilation with historic empathy, presenting the issues as they might have been perceived by people at that time. Students should be encouraged to question whether issues are ever as clear when we experience them as they are in retrospect.

This may also be a good place to explore the whole concept of revisionist history— the reinterpretation of past events to suit the political demands of the present. Current protests over celebrations honoring Columbus, DeSoto, and others are an example of this concept. Students might want to debate the legitimacy of this concept.

Analysis: [Compare the Cherokee to a plains tribe such as the Apache or the Sioux. Decide why the Cherokee tribe was called "civilized" and the other wasn't.] Answers will vary but should discuss, at least in part, the idea that the "civilized" tribes accepted (assimilated) some measure of white culture.

Students may be interested to learn that despite being regarded by many whites as naked barbarians, the Cherokee were fairly advanced on many cultural fronts. Marriage was monogamous. Intermarriage

within the tribe was forbidden (perhaps a factor in assimilation). Divorce was rare, but required only mutual consent. Laws were simple but rigidly enforced. Justice was likewise simple—an eye for an eye—and should a person flee to escape punishment, a kinsman was punished instead. (Interested students might want to learn more about the obligations this type of justice placed on the individual. A good example for discovery is Tsali, whose surrender saved the eastern Cherokee who today live on the Qualla Reservation in North Carolina.) Women were influential in the decision-making processes of the tribe, providing a contrast to the role of women in white culture.

Synthesis: [Speculate on how a governmental structure might have made it easier for the Cherokee to resist encroachment by the white man. Present your ideas on a poster or chart.] Valuing their independence highly, the Cherokee had no central governing body. Having nearly forty tribal groups within the Cherokee nation made coming to agreement on any central issue an overwhelming task. (One of the few times national law was enacted, enforcement almost split the nation in two: the Cherokee passed a law in 1829 that anyone who sold Cherokee lands to the Americans would be put to death. When the Treaty of New Echota was signed, each of its principal signers was condemned to death. This action split the nation almost as disastrously as the removal had.)

Evaluation: [The Cherokee Indian Removal Act was a clear example of the breakdown of America's checks and balances system. Decide who was the more civilized—the Cherokee or the United States. Support your decision.] Relevant facts might include the role of the Indian agents on the reservation, the treatment of Native Americans by traders along the Trails of Tears, and the constant breaking of treaties by the U.S. government. Twice before the Indian removal, the Indians sought remedies through the U.S. court system. Twice the Supreme Court upheld the Cherokee nation's claim to their land. However, the state of Georgia ignored the court's decisions and the president refused to allow federal troops to enforce them, choosing instead to use the troops to effect the maneuvers.

FOR FURTHER STUDY

Students might like to learn more about the Keetoowah, a secret society organized in 1859 to preserve Cherokee culture and independence.

Students could also investigate the ignominious treatment of other tribes and the suffering they endured. Of particular interest may be the story of the Nez Perce retreat.

Students may also wish to look at the place in society that Native Americans have today.

CONNECTING TO LITERATURE

Students might enjoy reading Harold Keith's *Rifles for Watie* and Lois Gladys Leppard's Mandy series of books (*Mandy* and the Secret Tunnel, Mandy and the Cherokee Legend, etc.).

The Mexican War

Purpose

As a result of completing the activities on this Bloom sheet, the students will demonstrate growth in the following areas:

1. explaining how a location's significance changes as cultures alter their interactions;

2. evaluating heroes and heroism based on criteria established by the students;

3. oral skills;

4. recognizing that there are multiple possible interpretations of any historical event.

5. speculating on differences that might have resulted had another point of view prevailed; and

6. demonstrating a knowledge of place and location by creating a map.

Knowledge: [Map the disputed territory of Texas, being sure to label the Nueces, Guadalupe, and Rio Grande rivers and to plot Santa Anna's route, Urrea's route, and Houston's route. Mark the location of the Alamo and of the battle of San Jacinto.] Textbooks or encyclopedias should be available for student use and for verifying responses.

Comprehension: [Write the script of a political debate between Clay and Polk on the issue of Manifest Destiny. Enlist the help of a classmate to present your skit to the class.] Essential differences include Clay's idea that change should come slowly, in contrast to Polk's eagerness to expand immediately. Clay also feared war with both Britain and Mexico. Polk welcomed such a possibility, proposing the acquisition of both Texas and Oregon to above the 54th parallel. "Fifty-four Forty or Fight" became the rallying cry of Polk's supporters, but a treaty compromising on the 49th parallel as Oregon's northern boundary kept us from entering another war with Britain.

Application: [You are an abolitionist angry over the possible acquisition of another slave state (Texas), over "Mr. Polk's War," over the Alamo. Design a "Wanted" poster calling for President Polk's arrest for "war crimes."] Products will vary. It might be worthwhile to try to obtain outdated "Wanted" posters from the post office or from local law enforcement agencies. We suggest that you screen these carefully to ascertain their appropriateness for your classroom.

Analysis: [Design a poster showing the terms of Slidell's proposal and the terms of the Treaty of Guadalupe-Hidalgo. Other than the loss of life suffered, what did Mexico lose by refusing to meet with Slidell?] Responses will vary. Major differences were the following:

Slidell's proposal had offered $25 million for Northern California and New Mexico and $5 million for the disputed land in Texas and had offered to cancel all claims for compensation for American citizens' property losses due to Mexican revolutions.

The treaty's proviso offered only $15 million for the same lands but included the cancellation of all claims for compensation.

The United States gained 525,000 square miles of territory as a result of the treaty, but the cost was two years of conflict and major loss of life. With the land came responsibility for 80,000 Mexican residents, who were offered American citizenship.

Analysis: [Make a sketch or model of the Alamo. How does this American fort compare to a medieval castle? Theorize as to why Americans built forts instead of castles. Present your findings to the class.] Responses will vary. Have students consider such factors as raw materials, sources of labor, immediacy of danger, style of fighting, and weapons available.

PUMP PRIMER ————

It is important that students recognize that though the battle at the Alamo took place nearly eleven years before the start of the war, its infamy lived on. Aware of the ignominious defeat, so many men tried to enlist when war was declared with Mexico that recruiting offices were jammed for days. "Remember the Alamo" became the battle cry of the Mexican War.

Synthesis: [Design a war monument honoring either the 187 Americans or the 1,550 Mexicans who died during the 13-day siege of the Alamo. Include an "inscription" explaining why

these men are being honored.] Responses will vary.

PUMP PRIMER ————

Students may never have considered that the Mexican soldiers who died at the Alamo were heroes—in their own country. Students at this age tend to see things as black-and-white and to consider Americans the heroes in every conflict. However, another point of view says that America was the aggressor here and the Mexicans were simply defending their property as well as the estimated 80,000 Mexican citizens who lived within the territories the United States acquired.

Evaluation: [William Barrett Travis, Jim Bowie, and Davy Crockett were heroes long before they came together in San Antonio. Evaluate what you know or can learn about these three men and decide which was the greatest hero. Support your choice in a paper or on a poster.] Travis's fame was largely due to his army career; he had risen to the rank of lieutenant colonel by the time of his death. Bowie had made famous the 8×1.5-inch knife designed by his older brother and used by Jim Bowie in hand-to-hand combat. Crockett had won fame as a Tennessee woodsman and had served two terms in the U.S. House of Representatives.

PUMP PRIMER ————

Students who became interested in the Mexican point of view in the synthesis task might prefer to research and choose among Mexican heroes such as

Santa Anna, Arista, and Doniphan.

EXTENDING THE STUDY

General Winfield Scott, whose capture of Mexico City effectively ended the Mexican War, was a hero to a later general, General Douglas MacArthur. Have students explore the similarities between these two men and their military careers and present their findings to the class. (MacArthur's landing at Inchon and recapture of Seoul during the Korean Conflict is often compared favorably with Scott's conquest of Mexico City. Both men seemed to have trouble accepting orders from the president of the United States. Both were eventually recalled, Scott by Polk and MacArthur by Truman.)

ADDITIONAL TEACHER RESOURCES

Spellman, Linda. *Castles, Codes, Calligraphy.* The Learning Works Enrichment Series, Santa Barbara, Calif.: The Learning Works, Inc., 1984.

Smith, A. G. *Castles of the World Coloring Book.* New York: Dover Publications, Inc., 1986.

The Gold Rush

Purpose

As a result of completing the activities on this Bloom sheet, the students will demonstrate growth in the following areas:

1. oral skills;
2. explaining the impact of an individual on historical development;
3. increasing awareness of the effect of a shared "secret";
4. relating economic and political conditions to historical change;
5. identifying the appropriate source to obtain information using print materials and technology; and
6. explaining how a location's significance changes as cultures alter their interactions.

Knowledge: [Describe the events leading up to the discovery of gold in California. Be sure to include information on James Marshall and John Sutter.] James Marshall, a carpenter, was working for John Sutter, a wealthy landowner. Marshall discovered gold near a mill that was being built in 1848. He took the gold nuggets to Sutter. They performed different tests until they reached the conclusion that they had found gold.

Comprehension: [Explain what a secret is and how to keep one. Suggest reasons why the men involved in the gold discovery could not keep a secret.] Answers will vary.

PUMP PRIMER ————————

Paul Tournier's small book *Secrets*, while too scholarly for most transescent students, might prove a good source for you in terms of directing discussion. The book outlines developmental stages of learning to keep

secrets and then of learning which ones to tell and when to tell them.

Comprehension: [Suggest reasons why the population of California in 1848, approximately 800, grew to 25,000 in 1850.] Students will undoubtedly decide that the lure of gold was enough to increase the population. However, many people had a keen sense of business and knew they could make money by supplying the miners with food and goods. The average person did not have the equipment necessary to do mining below the surface, but people chose to remain, primarily because of the climate. The increase in population contributed to California's achievement of statehood in 1850.

Application: [Prepare a pantomime depicting panning for gold.] Presentations will vary.

PUMP PRIMER ————————

The concept of panning for gold can be expanded into a lesson in values and/or self-concept: in order to reach the gold, miners had to sift through endless mounds of dirt and sand and had to learn the difference between pyrite (fool's gold) and gold. Ask students to generalize from this to other worthwhile things in life: for instance, in establishing friendships, is it necessary to sift through many relationships and to distinguish true friends from fair-weather friends? Allow students to brainstorm the names of other "valuables" that may be disguised in look-alikes and dross. Ask whether things worth having are worth the effort of mining them.

Discuss whether the good in ourselves is also usually hidden in a lot of phoniness and dross, and whether it's worth the effort to find that good.

Analysis: [Research what happened to John Sutter after his initial discovery. Did he live "happily ever after"? Explain.] John Sutter's property was in ruins after the gold rush. The miners' frenzy over gold caused them to lose respect for other people's property. John Sutter's land was destroyed, animals were killed, fences were knocked down, and buildings were dismantled and removed.

Synthesis: [Suppose you were eager to reach the gold mines of the West. Consider the three major means of travel available to reach your destination. Which method would you choose, and why?] You may wish to list the three primary modes of travel to the West during the gold rush: traveling by covered wagon across the Great Plains and Rocky Mountains, traveling by ship down and around the southern tip of South America, and taking a ship to the Isthmus of Panama, crossing land, and then going by sea to San Francisco.

Evaluation: [Criticize the greed evident during the gold rush of 1849. Include your opinion about the cost of food and supplies, as well as the disregard for the land.] This calls for an opinion based on the students' personal viewpoints and beliefs. This would be an excellent topic for discussion after papers have been turned in for evaluation. Depending on your location, some students may have had personal experience with price gouging. After Hurricane Andrew in 1992 and the flooding along the Mississippi in 1993, for example, many people tried to make money off the misery of others.

CONNECTING TO LITERATURE

For additional information, students might enjoy reading Kathryn Lasky's *Beyond the Divide*.

Communication

Purpose

As a result of completing the activities on this Bloom sheet, the students will demonstrate growth in the following areas:

1. identifying inventions that aided communication in the 1800s;

2. demonstrating an understanding of the Morse Code; and

3. interpreting changes made by individuals and events and how these changes can begin a new era in history.

Knowledge: [Match the following inventors with their inventions:]

Bell	telephone
Field	ocean floor cable
Hoe	rotating printing press
Morse	telegraph

Comprehension: [Rearrange the inventions in the "Knowledge" box in chronological order.]

1835	telegraph
1845	rotating print press
1866	ocean floor cable (Atlantic Cable)
1876	telephone

These dates reflect the first recorded patent or the first use of the invention. Other sources may use other dates. For example, 1844, the date of the first public message ("What hath God wrought?"), is the date more commonly given the telegraph, though patents predated that message. Conversely, the first patent for the rotary printing press was not granted until 1847. Despite these variances, the order will probably not change, but differences in dates may provoke some interesting speculation and debate among students.

Application: [Locate a list of the signals Samuel F. B. Morse used in the Morse code. Create a message using the code. Exchange with a classmate and translate each other's messages.] Answers will vary. Encyclopedias are a good reference source for the Morse code.

Analysis: [Determine the benefits of the telegraph.] There were several benefits to improving communication in the United States. Personal messages could travel more quickly. People were able to be informed of important news items faster. Businesses were able to expand. Railroad dispatches were easier to complete, and travel was made safer.

Synthesis: [Invent a new means of communication for the twenty-first century. Include a drawing or a description and an explanation of how it works.] Answers will vary.

Evaluation: [Grade the inventions developed by your peers. Base your decision on creativity and thoroughness.] You may wish to develop a form to be completed by students. You could list criteria for assigning a grade or students could generate a list of criteria for judging.

PUMP PRIMER

Many of the inventions of this period were actually conceived by African Americans, but the credit usually went to a white male. Have students investigate the role of all minorities in the inventions that changed the face of America.

CONNECTING TO READING, CRITICAL THINKING, AND ADVISORY TIME

Students are often fascinated by codes. Since encoding and decoding are basic reading skills, this might be a good avenue to providing practice without making it a drill exercise. You could suggest that students find examples of other codes, starting with simple substitution codes. Students could also create their own codes and try to break each other's codes. Cryptograms are also good practice. If you want to make breaking a code less frustrating, students need to be reminded of the structure of most English-language words:

each syllable usually has one vowel (or vowel sound), with *e* being the most frequently used vowel; *t, s,* and *d* are frequent word-ending consonants; one-letter words are usually *a* or *i*; two- and three-letter words are a good place to start looking for patterns; double-letter words are also a good starting place.

ADDITIONAL RESOURCES

Spellman, Linda, *Castles, Codes, Calligraphy* (The Learning Works, Inc., 1984).

The Underground Railroad

Purpose

As a result of completing the activities on this Bloom sheet, the students will demonstrate growth in the following areas:

1. distinguishing between facts and opinions;

2. demonstrating an understanding of human rights, concerns, and standards;

3. evaluating the effectiveness of one person acting as an agent for social change; and

4. oral skills.

Knowledge: [Read a biography of Harriet Tubman. In a group with two or three others, list as many facts as you can recall.] Many middle grades literature books contain excerpts from Ann Petry's *Harriet Tubman: Conductor on the Underground Railroad.* Other titles relevant to this sheet include Arna Bontemps'

Frederick Douglass: Slave, Fighter, Freeman; John Hope Franklin's *From Slavery to Freedom;* and William L. Katz's *Eyewitness: The Negro in American History.* Encyclopedias and history survey texts also are a source of biographies.

Comprehension: [Using your knowledge list, cluster the facts under two headings: the Underground Railroad and Harriet Tubman.] Clusters will vary.

Application: [Investigate the major route(s) traveled by "passengers" on the Underground Railroad. Trace the route(s) on a map of the northeastern United States.] The route described by Petry went from Dorchester, Maryland, through Wilmington, Delaware; Philadelphia, Pennsylvania; and Burlington, New Jersey; along the Hudson and Mohawk Rivers; through Syracuse and Rochester, New York, to St. Catherine's, Ontario (West Canada), Canada. Other routes may be discovered by students, but after promulgation of the Fugitive Slave Law, routes that had formerly ended in the free states of necessity extended into some part of Canada.

Analysis: [Two major analogies were employed in naming the slaves' escape mode: the routes' being called "the Underground Railroad" and Harriet Tubman's being called "Moses." Illustrate the parallels evident in these analogies.] Petry notes that Harriet Tubman was called the Moses of her people, partly to disguise her gender and partly because of these very obvious parallels. Make sure the following are noted: underground = secret (as an underground news-

paper); railroad = a mode of transportation; stations = stops for layovers; conductors = guides or leaders; passengers = escaping slaves; Moses = Harriet Tubman; both led their people from slavery to freedom; both were pursued and risked death if caught; both were deeply religious; both overcame physical handicaps (Moses was believed to have a speech impediment of some kind; Tubman was reputed to have a kind of epilepsy or narcolepsy).

Synthesis: [Compose a sentence that presents the philosophy that spawned the Underground Railroad and guided people like Harriet Tubman. Then reduce your own guiding philosophy of life to one sentence.] Philosophies will vary.

Evaluation: [Prepare oral arguments for debate on one side of the following topic: People have a moral obligation to break immoral laws.] Tell students that their conclusions should be based on, but not necessarily limited to, their knowledge of the underground railroad, abolition, and the Fugitive Slave Act. More capable students might want to prepare both sides of the question and actually stage the debate.

Evaluation: [Compare Harriet Tubman's contribution to the freedom movement with that of any four other leaders of movements. Decide which of the five was most influential or important. Make a presentation in which you justify your choice.]

Suggest that students choose from a list such as this:

Crispus Attucks

John Brown

Anthony Burns

Frederick Douglass

W. E. B. DuBois

Charles G. Finney

Thomas Garrett

William Lloyd Garrison

Sarah and Angelina Grimke

Rev. J. W. Loguen

Wendell Phillips

Dred Scott

Harriet Beecher Stowe

Aurthur and Lewis Tappan

Nat Turner

Theodore Weld

Other historical figures to investigate might include Socrates, Thoreau, Gandhi, and Martin Luther King.

CONNECTING TO LITERATURE

Students might enjoy reading Conrad Stein's *The Story of the Underground Railroad* for more background.

CONNECTING TO MUSIC

Students might like to investigate the role of spirituals in the freedom movement. They might look at the spiritual from the viewpoints of unifying the people, of overcoming illiteracy, of boosting morale, and of granting religious sanction to illegal acts. Have them discuss why some spirituals were banned.

The Civil War

Purpose

As a result of completing the activities on this Bloom sheet,

the students will demonstrate growth in the following areas:

1. explaining the impact of an individual on historical development;

2. constructing a time line;

3. relating economic and political conditions to historical change; and

4. identifying the appropriate source to obtain information using print materials and technology.

Knowledge: [Describe the events leading up to the Civil War.] Answers may include Stowe's portrayal of slavery in *Uncle Tom's Cabin*; the differences between the North and South in industry, commerce, way of life, government, and politics; and two questions of great concern: Should slavery be expanded into the new territories? Are independent states more powerful than the Union?

Comprehension: [Explain how the Civil War ended. Include names of those involved, locations, and other specific details.] Grant led the northern army toward Richmond. Grant's army took control of an important rail center and controlled roads leading into and out of Richmond. By 1865, the Union army controlled the Confederate capital. Lee's troops were in a poor state and they surrendered at Appomattox Court House, Virginia.

Application: [Choose three of the following and describe their roles in the Civil War: General Ulysses S. Grant, General William T. Sherman, General Robert E. Lee, Jefferson Davis, Abra-

ham Lincoln, General Thomas J. Jackson.] Grant led the Union armies during the final years of the war. Sherman led the Union army into Georgia. Lee commanded the Confederate Army of Northern Virginia. Davis was president of the Confederacy. Lincoln was president of the United States during the Civil War. Jackson (nicknamed "Stonewall") was commander of the Confederate Army.

Analysis: [Select five to ten key events of the Civil War and show them on a time line.] Answers will vary.

Synthesis: [Tell what might have happened had Abraham Lincoln not been shot.] Answers will vary.

Evaluation: [Research the assassination of Abraham Lincoln and debate the fairness of what happened to Booth, to the other conspirators, and to Dr. Samuel Mudd.] Responses will vary. Students might like to research Fort Jefferson in the Dry Tortugas, off the Florida Keys, and to learn about Dr. Mudd's imprisonment there.

ADDITIONAL TEACHER RESOURCES

Fletcher Pratt, *The Civil War in Pictures* (New York: Garden City Books, 1955.)

Students might enjoy reading the following:

Stephen Crane, *The Red Badge of Courage*

Virginia Hamilton, *The People Could Fly*

Irene Hunt, *Across Five Aprils*

Harold Keith, *Rifles for Watie*

Carl Sandburg, *Abraham Lincoln Grows Up*

Steve Sanfield, *The Adventures of High John, the Conqueror*

Abraham Lincoln

Purpose

As a result of completing the activities on this Bloom sheet, the students will demonstrate growth in the following areas:

1. oral skills;

2. developing and presenting interpretations about and comparisons of presidencies;

3. speculating on differences that might have resulted had another point of view prevailed; and

4. explaining the impact of an individual on historical development.

Knowledge: [Read a biography of Abraham Lincoln.] Responses will vary. Due to the varying ability levels of students and the amount of time you have to devote to this project, you may wish to allow students to self-select biographies or to use reference sources such as encyclopedias, biographical dictionaries, or magazines. You may prefer to duplicate a simplified one- or two-page biography. In a heterogeneous classroom, you might want to combine all three options. The key is to provide students with ample information to complete the study sheet without overwhelming them with reading.

Knowledge: [List ten major accomplishments of Abraham Lincoln.] Answers will vary. If your classroom has some notable task-avoidance wags, you may wish to prohibit entries such as the dates of his birth and death.

PUMP PRIMER

Students might wish to pool their lists, put them in chronological order, and make a wall chart or other suitable display for them. To connect to math, some students could tally the number of times each fact is mentioned by class members and graph the results. This could also lead to a "Top Ten" list based on class consensus.

PUMP PRIMER

An alternative to these knowledge tasks, especially effective with highly accomplished students, would be to ask the students to write a children's book about Lincoln. Recognize that such an assignment moves the activity to the synthesis level, but the completion of the activity will subsume the requirements of both knowledge tasks.

Two concerns you will need to deal with if students are to write a children's book are style and vocabulary.

Style becomes an issue with most transescent students, as they typically construct biography as a bred-fed-wed-led-dead sequence that is usually about as interesting as watching dishwater cool—a few spectacular bursts, but mostly just slow fizzle. Allow students some time to peruse a few children's biographies and analyze them. Point out that the most interesting ones usually

have an episodic format—they present brief, spaced anecdotes that give a picture of the person without covering an endless list of events.

Vocabulary is the second consideration: although young children may be inordinately proud of learning a word like *Constantinople* or *stegosaurus* when it appears in a book, a steady diet of such words changes the experience from challenge reading to frustration. You might want to provide students with a Dolch reading list or some other list of early-reading vocabulary words and have them devise a glossary for any words not on the list.

Comprehension: [Enlist the help of classmates to dramatize an incident from Lincoln's life. In your introduction, explain the significance of the incident.] Responses will vary. To avoid confusion and/or keep students from using too much class time, you may want to assign students to work groups and have them present their dramatization to their groups rather than to the entire class. If you desire, each work group could then choose one skit to be presented to the entire class.

PUMP PRIMER

Lincoln was affected by the strong influence of the women in his life: his mother, who died when Lincoln was young; his stepmother; and his wife, Mary Todd Lincoln. Students might want to examine the influence of women in the backgrounds of many of our presidents, including Lincoln, Franklin Roosevelt, and Bill Clinton.

Application: [Produce a pamphlet that shows the issues facing Lincoln as he assumed the presidency.] Responses will vary.

PUMP PRIMER

Some students may have difficulty starting this assignment. A possible solution might be to secure (perhaps with a call to a political headquarters) some campaign literature and use that as a springboard. Lincoln's stands on the various issues could be presented as campaign promises. This might be a good place to use the Me-2-3 Rule for cooperative learning. Under the rule, students can choose to work alone or with one or two partners of their own choosing. This provides a nice occasional alternative to random grouping and base groups.

Analysis: [Lincoln's life was full of irony and paradox, but the incidents that have received the most attention involve the remarkable resemblances to John F. Kennedy's life. Chart the parallels between the two presidents.] Responses will vary. Lincoln and Kennedy served terms in the U.S. House of Representatives beginning one hundred years apart and were elected president one hundred years apart, each after failing to be chosen vice president, also one hundred years apart. Their vice presidents, both named Johnson, were born one hundred years apart.

Each had a son die during his presidency: Lincoln's eleven-year-old son Willie and Kennedy's infant son Patrick both died of respiratory conditions.

Both men had been warned not to go to the place where they were eventually assassinated, Lincoln by an aide named Kennedy, and Kennedy by an aide named Lincoln. Both presidents were shot in the head from behind on a Friday.

Their assassins, John Wilkes Booth and Lee Harvey Oswald, were Southerners who were shot to death before they could be brought to trial.

PUMP PRIMER

Other than the ironies of comparison that students may discover, both men had many personal ironies that often intrigue students. For example, Lincoln's son Robert Todd fell from a train platform in 1864 and was in danger of being killed by an approaching train when he was rescued by Edwin Booth—the brother of the man who a year later shot Lincoln. And although John F. Kennedy was a champion of civil rights, especially with regard to the Negro, there lived another John Kennedy, John B. Kennedy, a Confederate veteran from Tennessee, who was one of the organizers of the Ku Klux Klan.

Synthesis: [Speculate on how Reconstruction might have been different had Lincoln not been assassinated. Give at least five ways in which things would have been different.] Responses will vary, but speculation about what Lincoln might have done should not contradict the tenets of his Ten Percent Plan.

Evaluation: [Lincoln overcame poverty, obscurity, and lack of formal schooling to become one of America's most revered presidents. List in order of importance the eight to ten factors you feel were most responsible for his success. Give reasons for your choices.] Responses will vary.

CONNECTING TO LITERATURE

Students may wish to read and/or memorize Lincoln's "Gettysburg Address," perhaps the most famous speech of its length ever made. Students might want to compare it with Douglas's speech, both in length and content. This is also a good time to look at the literature this president inspired, from Walt Whitman's "Oh, Captain, My Captain" to Carl Sandburg's multivolume biography. Students might speculate on what it was about Lincoln that inspired such a massive body of literature.

Reconstruction

Purpose

As a result of completing the activities on this Bloom sheet, the students will demonstrate growth in the following areas:

1. relating economic and political conditions to historical change;

2. using a graphic organizer to summarize information;

3. perceiving events and issues as they were experienced by people living at that time to develop historic empathy as opposed to present-mindedness.

4. oral skills; and

5. identifying similarities and differences in dissimilar data.

Knowledge: [Generate a list of problems facing Americans after the Confederate surrender at Appomattox Courthouse. On a chart, combine your list with that of classmates.] Among the facts for consideration are the following:

- The African American population was largely penniless, homeless, and illiterate, and it faced white animosity.

- Confederate soldiers were largely emaciated, sick, and handicapped, and often were homeless.

- Many men belonged to both groups, which multiplied their problems.

- Many cities had been burned, looted, or destroyed.

- Often families had been divided and family members had fought on opposing sides, leaving them no supportive family to whom to return.

- Railroad tracks, factories, and businesses had been destroyed.

- Money was worthless.

Comprehension: [Assume the role of a newly freed person who has traveled to Abilene to start a new life. In a series of letters to and from your mother who is still in Mississippi, describe what life is like for African Americans both in the West and in the South. Be sure to write your letters in first person.] Answers will vary. Students should under-stand that while there were significant differences in prospects in these two places, neither picture was very attractive.

Application: [Using overlapping circles, draw an illustration of the major plans for reconstruction: the Presidential (Ten Percent) Plan, the Wade-Davis Bill, the Reconstruction Act, and Johnson's Plan (Presidential Restoration Plan). Use the overlapped area to illustrate any points these plans had in common.] Answers will vary.

Analysis: [Explain why rebuilding after the War between the States was so much more massive a project than rebuilding after other wars. Give at least five reasons.] Possible reasons include the following:

1. The war had lasted for five years.

2. The war was fought entirely on U.S. soil.

3. The war had divided families, communities, and churches.

4. Lincoln's assassination caused a realigning of loyalties.

5. Reconstruction issues were not addressed in the Constitution.

Synthesis: [Compose a skit, song, poem, or story about the scalawags and carpetbaggers.] Products will vary.

Evaluation: [Estimate the effects of a half century of American life under *Plessy v. Ferguson* and the effects of *Brown v. Board of Education of Topeka*. Which ruling do you believe was the more significant? Give reasons. How might life be different today had the "separate but equal" principle never been in place?] Answers will vary. Remind students that *Plessy v. Ferguson* established the doctrine of separate but equal facilities. *Brown* overturned it.

Westward, Ho!

Purpose

As a result of completing the activities on this Bloom sheet, the students will demonstrate growth in the following areas:

1. explaining how and why people moved themselves, their products, and their ideas across America;

2. applying knowledge of place and location to demonstrate an understanding of human interdependence;

3. relating economic and political conditions to historical change;

4. identifying the belief system inherent in a culture as revealed in the traits of its heroes;

5. utilizing appropriate geographical, reference/study, and critical thinking skills to make decisions and solve a problem; and

6. identifying likenesses and differences in dissimilar data.

Knowledge: [Read a biography of an American trailblazer. List eight facts that make him or her important as a trailblazer.] While you may want to encourage able students to read books, students could just as easily read encyclopedia or biographical dictionary entries. They could also do their reading and listing in cooperative groups.

PUMP PRIMER

Prewriting discussion might center around the question What makes a trailblazer important? Such brainstorming might keep students from listing irrelevancies such as where, when, and to whom a trailblazer was born. Overemphasis on selection criteria, however, raises this from a knowledge question to an evaluation question and may not be appropriate for students whose ability level is average or below.

Suggested trailblazers:

William Becknell
James P. Beckwourth
Daniel Boone
Jim Bridger
Christopher (Kit) Carson
Toussaint Charbonneau
Jesse Chisholm
George Rogers Clark
William Clark
John Charles Fremont
Meriwether Lewis
John Marshall
Joseph Nicollet
Zebulon Pike
Sacagawea
Father Junipero Serra
Jedediah Smith
Eliza Spaulding
Jesse Reddeford Walker
Marcus Whitman
Narcissa Whitman

Comprehension: [On a map, label each of the following trails and, where possible, the explorer who opened it: El Camino Real, the Chisholm Trail, the Trail of Tears, the Oregon Trail, the Natchez Trace, the Cumberland (National) Road, the Santa Fe Trail, the Spanish Trail, the Butterfield Overland Mail Route, the Mohawk Trail, the Wilderness Road, and the Goodnight Loving Trail.] Decide ahead of time how much accuracy is required for full credit.

Application: [With two or three classmates, draw up a list of problems you might encounter on a trip west in 1872. Decide what supplies you would need in order to be prepared for these eventualities.] Students who have played Oregon Trail from MECC software, Wagons West from Scholastic, or other such computer simulations will have some idea where to start. If this group is small, make them your "experts" who help the others. If there are no students who have played these games, you may want to start by brainstorming with the entire class.

PUMP PRIMER

Consider fundamental needs such as water, food, shelter, warmth, and so on first. Move to manufactured products not available on the trail (clothing, for example). Next consider possible disasters—diseases, broken wagons, tornados, floods, Indian attacks. Finally consider more esoteric things like recreation, companionship, and the like.

Analysis: [List similarities and differences between Western trailblazers and world explorers

such as Marco Polo and space explorers such as Neil Armstrong and Sally Ride.] Some students might be interested in extending this activity to include other types of pioneers—in medicine, in speed, in science. Encourage them to present their findings on a poster or videotape, so others may learn from their efforts.

Synthesis: [Examine some of the folk heroes, tall tales, and legends that arose during the westward expansion of our nation. Create a new character and write some tall tales about him or her. Use this person's exploits to explain physical features of the land or natural phenomena.] Direct students toward such characters as Pecos Bill, Paul Bunyan, Mike Fink, Stormalong, and Joe Magarac, as well as toward real heroes like Johnny Appleseed (John Chapman), Davy Crockett, Casey Jones, Sam Houston, and Daniel Boone.

Evaluation: [Investigate the importance to westward expansion of gold, free land, Indian relocation, religious oppression, civil war, industrialization, and the open range. Rank these in order from most influential to least influential. Give reasons for your choices.] This activity could easily be the unit test, since it requires the student to draw on knowledge from everything covered.

CONNECTING TO LITERATURE

Among the numerous books about life in America's West available for students to enjoy are these:

Carol Ryrie Brink, *Caddie Woodlawn*

Patricia MacLachlan, *Sarah, Plain and Tall*

Jack Schaefer, *Shane*

Laura Ingalls Wilder, *Little House on the Prairie* and its sequels

ADDITIONAL TEACHER RESOURCES

Klawitter, Pamela Amick. *Pirates, Explorers, Trailblazers*, Learning Works Enrichment Series. Santa Barbara, Calif.: The Learning Works, Inc., 1987.

Kovacs, Deborah. Wagons West: A Twistaplot™ Adventure (software). *Microzine*, No. 12 (Scholastic, Inc., 1985).

Oregon Trail. Minnesota Educational Computing Corporation, 1985.

"Oregon Trail: The Itch to Move West." *National Geographic*, Vol. 170, No. 2 (Aug., 1986), p. 147–177.

Cowboys

Purpose

As a result of completing the activities on this Bloom sheet, the students will demonstrate growth in the following areas:

1. consolidating information from many sources into a new product;

2. articulating the cowboys' influence on and contribu-

tions to America's national heritage;

3. describing the various roles of cowboys and how they changed over time; and

4. oral skills.

Knowledge: [Define the following: chaps, lasso, rodeo, wrangler, trail drive, bandanna, poncho, sombrero, Western saddle.]

chaps: strong, seatless leather leggings

lasso: a long rope or line of hide or other material with a noose at one end, used for roping cattle, horses, and so on

rodeo: competition set up to demonstrate cowboy skills such as bronco riding and calf roping

wrangler: boy or man who cared for the saddle ponies that traveled with a trail outfit

trail drive: organized movement of great herds of cattle across prairies to market

bandanna: cotton or silk handkerchief usually worn around the cowboy's neck

poncho: blanket-like cloak having an opening for the head

sombrero: large straw or felt hat with a broad brim and a high crown

Western saddle: leather seat for a rider characterized by a horn used for securing ropes

Comprehension: [Describe what life was like on the open range.] One good source that appears in many middle school literature texts is J. Frank Dobie's essay "The Bandanna."

Application: [Prepare a presentation that gives five or more facts about the life of a well-known cowboy.] Answers will vary. If your book lists no cowboys by name, allow students to choose from the following: Buffalo Bill Cody, Wild Bill Hickok, John Wesley Hardin, Commodore Perry Owens, Jesse James, Billy the Kid, J. Frank Dobie, Charles Russell, or Wyatt Earp.

Analysis: [Illustrate a scene in the West of 1800.] Elements you may want students to include are store fronts, mining towns, water supplies, stables, a smithy, and so on. If students are anxious about their artistic abilities, you might want to allow them to work in pairs, giving one the responsibility for the research and decision-making (and possibly a written summary of what is in the illustration) while the other takes on the task of drawing and coloring.

Analysis: [Compare the cowboy as he is portrayed in your social studies text with the cowboys who appeared in fictional stories or in television programs and movies. What conclusions can be drawn from your comparison?] Students wanting to read cowboy stories might consider Jack Schaefer's *Shane*, the stories of Louis L'Amour, and/or the stories of Zane Grey.

Synthesis: [Create a poem, skit, or rap song about the cowboy.] Products will vary.

Evaluation: [Defend today's use of trucks, jeeps, and even helicopters to round up cattle instead of the traditional use of horses.] Students should consider speed, comfort, number of hands required, availability of telephones or radios, among their things.

CONNECTING TO ART

Students might enjoy learning more about cowboy artists such as Frederick Remington and Charlie Russell and about photographic chroniclers of the West such as F. Jay Haynes and Charles Belden.

CONNECTING TO MUSIC

Students may tend to think of modern country music when asked to discuss western music, but western cowboy music is a distinct sound, different from country/western. Students might enjoy listening to some of the cowboy songs and range ballads available on a variety of cassettes, records, and compact discs. They may want to extend their exploration to some of the singing cowboys made famous by Hollywood, such as Gene Autry, Roy Rogers, and Tex Ritter. Contemporary country/western artist Chris LeDoux has recorded several albums of western music including *Paint Me Back Home in Wyoming, Cowboys Ain't Easy to Love,* and *Sounds of the Western Country.* Other recent artists include Liz Masterson and Don Edwards.

CONNECTING TO ENVIRONMENTAL ISSUES

Students may not realize that the Tipi (also spelled *tepee*) was used by various plains tribes because it did not harm the land and because it was easily transportable once the planting season was over. The same land was not usually used year after year by native Americans, as it was by whites, because the Indians recognized that the land needed time to replenish itself if it was to support farm life. Have students explore other native American customs that indicate that the Indian understood the laws of nature much better than did the encroaching cowboy "civilization."

CONNECTING TO HOME ECONOMICS

Students might enjoy investigating rangeland cooking and the historical context of the field. City dwellers and noncampers may never have considered the importance to our culture of refrigeration and microwave cooking, or what life without them must have been like.

CONNECTING TO LANGUAGE ARTS

There are nine museums whose collective efforts are dedicated to preserving the history, art, and culture of the American West. Encourage students to write to the nearest of these museums and inquire about exhibitions, special programs, and products that may be available locally. The museums are the Buffalo Bill Historical Center, Cody, Wyoming; the Eiteljorg Museum, Indianapolis, Indiana; the Gene Autry Western Heritage Museum, Los Angeles, California; the Gilcrease Museum, Tulsa, Oklahoma; the Glenbow Museum, Calgary, Alberta, Canada; the Heard Museum, Phoenix, Arizona; the Millicent Rogers Museum, Taos, New Mexico; the National Cowboy Hall of Fame, Oklahoma City, Oklahoma; and the Rockwell Museum, Corning, New York.

ADDITIONAL TEACHER RESOURCES

"C. M. Russell, Cowboy Artist." *National Geographic,* Vol. 169, No. 1 (Jan. 1986), pp. 60–95.

Freedman, Russell. *Cowboys of the Wild West.* New York: Clarion Books, 1985.

Matthews, Leonard J. *The Wild West in American History: Gunfighters.* Vero Beach, Fla.: Rourke Publications, Inc., 1989.

The Women's West. edited and with an introduction by Susan Armitage and Elizabeth Jameson. Available from The Buffalo Bill Historical Center, P.O. Box 2630, Cody, Wyoming 82414.

Indians

Purpose

As a result of completing the activities on this Bloom sheet, the students will demonstrate growth in the following areas:

1. utilizing globes or maps as primary geography tools;

2. demonstrating an understanding of universal human rights, concerns, and standards;

3. identifying likenesses in and differences between modern society and a historic culture; and

4. speculating on the development of future civilizations based on the influence and contributions of past events.

Knowledge: [List the five American Indian tribes that actively participated in the Civil War. Discover whether these tribes still exist today.] Five American Indian tribes took a direct part in the Civil War: the Choctaw, the Chickasaw, the Creek, the Seminole, and the Cherokee. The Choctaw and the Chickasaw were united in their support of the South. The Creek, the Seminole, and the Cherokee were divided. A Cherokee named Stand Watie became a general in the Confederate Army. These tribes were moved to "The Territory" (principally in what is now Oklahoma) and still exist today.

Comprehension: [On a map of the United States, locate the following reservations: Rosebud, the Colorado River, and Pine Ridge.] Pine Ridge and Rosebud are in South Dakota; the Colorado River, in Arizona. You may wish to require students to map the locations of any tribes that are or were in your area as well.

Application: [Make a replica of an Indian village.] Most villages were near a water supply. Depending on the tribe selected, students will want to include teepees or other dwellings, mounds, irrigation canals (used by the Hohokam and other tribes), pueblos, kivas, wickiups, and so on.

Analysis: [Contrast the life of a Native American living on a reservation now with reservation life in the 1800s.] Students should investigate the experi-

ence of Native Americans today, including the effects of alcohol and unemployment, and compare their educational opportunities with those of whites. Students might enjoy reading the excerpt "It Will Not Be Seen Again" from N. Scott Momaday's *The Names,* or his *House Made of Dawn* or *The Way to Rainy Mountain,* and making this material the basis for this report. Edgar Wyatt's *Cochise, Apache Warrior and Statesman* is also good.

This is a good place to teach or reemphasize graphic organizers. If the science or math department teaches Venn Diagrams and you want to reinforce their use, instruct students to *compare* and contrast using the Venn model.

Synthesis: [Predict what life would be like for Native Americans if they had not been made to live on reservations.] Responses will vary.

Evaluation: [Describe life as you see it for the Native American in the next century.] Responses will vary.

CONNECTING TO LITERATURE

Among the numerous works of literature about native Americans available to be enjoyed by students are the following:

John Bierhorst, *Doctor Coyote: A Native American Aesop's Fables*

Walter D. Edwards, *The Matchlock Gun*

M. J. Wheeler, *First Came the Indians*

EXTENDING THE STUDY

Students might be interested in being pen pals with students in an American Indian school. Contact the Office of Indian Educational Programs, Bureau of Indian Affairs, Department of the Interior, Washington, DC 20240 for information. Write to the school to propose classroom-to-classroom exchanges of letters, photos, and the like. It is probably not wise to have students mail out letters at random before you have found another teacher willing to exchange. If the letters are sent to a school that is not interested in such an exchange or to one that has already established a link elsewhere, they may not respond to your students. Caution students, too, in writing to their pen pals, that they avoid phraseology that would be condescending or insulting. Exchanging cultural information with someone who is of the same nationality but from a different cultural background is different from an exchange with a student from a foreign country. Students need to be sensitive to this difference.

ADDITIONAL TEACHER RESOURCES

"C. M. Russell, Cowboy Artist" *National Geographic,* Vol. 169, No. 1 (Jan. 1986), pp. 60–95.

Western Outlaws and Lawmen

Purpose

As a result of completing the activities on this Bloom Sheet, the student will demonstrate growth in the following areas:

1. demonstrating the ability to locate, access, organize, and use information about public issues;

2. obtaining appropriate information from tables of contents, indices, encyclopedias, and other sources;

3. organizing information in visual and journalistic formats; and

4. identifying the appropriate source to obtain information using print materials and technology.

Knowledge: [Identify the following: Jesse James, Billy the Kid, Sam Bass, William B. Masterson, Wyatt Earp, Patrick Floyd Garrett, and Wild Bill Hickok.] Answers will vary, but may include the following information:

Jesse James (1847–1881). Born in Clay County, Missouri, Jesse James was the son of a Baptist minister. James was a bank and train robber who led robberies in Missouri as well as other states. Jesse and his brother, Frank, joined forces with their cousins, the Youngers.

Billy the Kid (1859–1881). Henry McCarty (later known as Billy the Kid) killed a man after a quarrel in 1877 and became a fugitive. He moved to New Mexico, where he changed his name to William H. Bonney. A rancher gave him a job and became his friend. After the death of his friend in 1878, the Kid started a career of cattle stealing and killing.

Sam Bass (1851–1878). Bass was known as the Robin Hood of Texas. He left home at the age of seventeen to become a cowboy and fell in with a bad crowd. He stole from the rich to give to the poor. He was killed by the Texas Rangers.

William B. Masterson (1853–1921). In his youth, Bat Masterson was a buffalo hunter and Indian fighter. He began his career as a peace officer in 1876. In 1881 he helped Wyatt Earp enforce the law in Tombstone, Arizona. In 1902, he became a sportswriter after moving to New York City.

Wyatt Earp (1848–1929). While a peace officer, Earp took part in the famous battle at the O.K. Corral. Born in Monmouth, Illinois., he led a varied life as a stagecoach driver, railroad construction hand, and surveyor.

Patrick Floyd Garrett (1850–1908). Born in Alabama, Garrett became a cowhand and buffalo hunter before becoming a sheriff of Lincoln County in 1880. Pat Garrett is credited with the capture and killing of Billy the Kid.

Wild Bill Hickok (1837–1876). Born James Butler Hickok in Troy Grove, Illinois, Wild Bill reportedly killed only in self-defense and in the line of duty. Hickok served as a scout for the Union Army during the Civil War. He later became a marshall in Kansas and toured with Buffalo Bill in 1872.

Comprehension: [Organize the facts from the knowledge activity on a mobile.] Products will vary.

PUMP PRIMER ─────────

Suggest to students that they paste a magazine picture on one side of each mobile shape and a fact on the other. If available, stencils or die cut pictures from your media center would offer students more shape options, such as horses, stagecoaches, railroad cars, or handguns.

Application: [Locate information on "dime novels." Record your findings as a television commercial or radio announcement.] Answers will vary, but may include the following: Dime novels were prevalent from 1860 to 1870. These stories portrayed a violent way of life that was meant to be entertaining. Images of the frontier provided a means of escaping from the everyday routine for the people living in the east. After the frontier was closed, the stories became more romantic. Dime novels were enjoyed by young and old.

Analysis: [Examine the terms *cattle rustler, train robber, hired gun, confidence man, cardsharp, claim jumper,* and *pickpocket.* Form generalizations about the character of a western outlaw.] Students should realize that the settlements in the West attracted many people who came only to cheat and steal. Cowboys looked forward to reaching a settlement after spending weeks on a trail drive. Students may need to define some terms: A *cardsharp* was a person who cheated at poker by using a deck of marked cards. A *claim jumper* was a person who illegally took over a mine claimed by another person. A *confidence man* was a swindler who often sold stock that proved to be worthless.

PUMP PRIMER

Although women were not as confined by social mores in the West as they had been in the East, there still were not a great number of women who gained fame (or infamy) as either outlaws or law enforcers. However, students might enjoy researching some of these more colorful characters, women such as Calamity Jane and Belle Starr.

Synthesis: [Design a "Wanted" poster for a fictitious outlaw. Include the facts necessary to inform the public about this person.] Products will vary.

Evaluation: [Decide if it is right to "take the law into your own hands." Support your decision with a minimum of three reasons. Express your opinion in a short essay.] Answers will vary.

Evaluation: [Decide if you are for or against the death penalty. Support your decision.] Answers will vary.

CONNECTING TO LANGUAGE ARTS

Students might wish to examine some biographies and biographical sketches of western outlaws and lawmen, trying to distinguish between fact and opinion. They might also investigate which of these men and women seemed larger than life as their legends outstripped their actual deeds, turning them into folk heroes.

CONNECTING TO DRAMA

View several western movies, TV shows, or broadway plays and discuss how the outlaws and lawmen were portrayed on the screen or stage. Have students determine whether these portrayals are any more accurate than those in the dime novels.

The Transcontinental Railroad

Purpose

As a result of completing the activities on this Bloom sheet, the students will demonstrate growth in the following areas:

1. naming the railroad lines responsible for the completion of the Transcontinental Railroad;

2. explaining the impact of an individual on historical development;

3. evaluating the quality of life before and after the completion of the Transcontinental Railroad;

4. demonstrating a knowledge of place and location by creating a map; and

5. explaining how a location's significance changes as cultures alter their interactions.

Knowledge: [Find the names of three railroad lines in the United States (past or present).] Possible answers include New York Central System, the Pennsylvania, the Erie, the Baltimore and Ohio, the Union and Pacific, and the Central Pacific.

Comprehension: [Trace on a map the development of the Transcontinental Railroad. Where did the lines meet?] The Union and Pacific began in Omaha, Nebraska, and moved west, and the Central Pacific began in Sacramento, California, and went east. The lines met at Ogden, Utah.

Application: [Discuss the improvements made to railroad comfort and safety by George Pullman and George Westinghouse.] George Pullman developed the sleeper car and the dining car. George Westinghouse was the man responsible for developing a braking system that could be applied in all of the railroad cars at the same time. Decide in advance whether you want this to be a written, small group oral, or whole class discussion.

Analysis: [Compare life in the West before and after the completion of the Transcontinental Railroad.] Prior to the building of the Transcontinental Railroad, railroad lines were short; they mainly connected large cities. Goods had to be removed from the railroad cars and loaded into wagons and then transported to the connecting line only to be loaded again. This was expensive and time-consuming. Because different companies built the railroad lines, tracks were different widths and not all trains could travel on them. After the Transcontinental Railroad was completed, it was possible to travel the country with ease and speed. It was a vast improvement in the transportation of merchandise.

PUMP PRIMER

Students may wish to investigate the difficulties faced by both the Union Pacific and Central Pacific Railroads in building the Transcontinental Railroad.

Synthesis: [Create a railroad scene. Turn a shoebox into a railroad car. Use toothpicks or popsicle sticks to create the railroad track. Use your imagination!] Work will vary. If you have students who have model trains at home, encourage them to present them to the class.

Evaluation: [Decide if train travel is still a useful form of transportation. Justify your decision with three reasons.] Answers will vary. Perhaps students will include a discussion on time as a factor in travel today.

CONNECTING TO MUSIC

Explore songs about rail travel. Include "The Atchison, Topeka, and the Santa Fe," "The Chattanooga Choo-Choo," and "The Orange Blossom Special" as well as more current songs, such as Arlo Guthrie's "City of New Orleans."

CONNECTING TO FOLKLORE

Discuss tales about Casey Jones, John Henry, and the golden spike.

ADDITIONAL RESOURCE

Cohn, Amy, ed. *From Sea to Shining Sea: A Treasury of American Folklore and Folk Songs.* Scholastic, 1993.

The Industrial Revolution

Purpose

As a result of completing the activities on this Bloom sheet, students will demonstrate growth in the following areas:

1. explaining the impact of an individual on historical development;

2. relating political and economic conditions to historical change;

3. using a graphic organizer to summarize information;

4. evaluating the effects on society of an individual belief system's differing from established law;

5. oral skills; and

6. speculating on differences that might have resulted had another point of view prevailed.

Knowledge: [Write a brief paragraph telling how each of these men contributed to the Industrial Revolution: Samuel F. B. Morse, Francis Cabot Lowell, Robert Fulton, Samuel Slater, and Eli Whitney.]

Samuel F. B. Morse was the inventor of the telegraph. His machine for sending encoded messages via electrical impulses revolutionized communication, affecting all areas of life, but especially journalism and railroads.

Francis Cabot Lowell is credited with the Lowell factory system, which employed children and young women to mass produce textiles in Lowell's Waltham, Massachusetts plant. Though the system was eventually criticized for its many abusive practices, at its inception, it provided a safe environment in dormitory living and employment for young unmarried women.

Robert Fulton is known as the inventor and developer of the steamboat, important for its low passenger and freight rates upriver, its speed, and its encouragement of westward expansion.

Samuel Slater was an English machinist who memorized the mechanical structure of a British spinning machine, disguised himself as farmer, booked passage to America, and built the first American spinning jenny. Though he may not have violated British copyright law, he violated its spirit: its intent had been to keep the machines in England and maintain a monopoly on the manufacturing process. The fact that he assumed a disguise to sneak out of the country attests to his awareness of what he was doing.

Eli Whitney contributed two things to the Industrial Revolution: a cotton gin and a manufacturing system based on interchangeable parts. The cotton gin mechanized and speeded up the tedious process of picking seeds out of cotton so that it could be used for spinning. Interchangeable parts meant that products no longer had to be produced one at a time (the lock, stock, and barrel approach) and a machine no longer had to be replaced in toto when it broke.

Comprehension: [Research American demographics in 1800. Use that information to write a paragraph describing what American life would have been like without industrialization.] Paragraphs will vary. In 1800 the U.S. had a population of about five million people in sixteen states, approximately sixty-five percent of whom lived within fifty miles of the Atlantic coast, the majority in rural areas. This region also encompassed most of the existing cities however. The cities were beginning to develop art and cultural centers, music halls, theaters, and public schools. However, the limited manufacturing that existed was insufficient to attract people from the farms and plantations or to provide jobs for the immigrants who arrived there.

Application: [Illustrate and label a machine that figured prominently in the Industrial Revolution.] Work will vary.

Analysis: [Working with a partner, plan a presentation to explain the effects on slavery of the invention of the cotton gin. Join another pair and take turns teaching the group.] Essential elements include these: the gin (short for engine) increased to fifty pounds the amount of cotton one worker could clean in a day, increasing total cotton production by 250 percent. As cotton became a more profitable crop, the demand for slaves

became more intense and the possibility that slaves would be freed grew increasingly more remote.

Analysis: [The development of the microchip has been cited as the beginning of a new industrial revolution. Use a graphic organizer to show how the shift from manual to mechanical labor was both like and different from the shift from industry to technology and robotics.] Answers will vary.

Synthesis: [Despite the changes brought by assembly lines, interchangeable parts, and other signs of mechanization, there still are those who enjoy making products the old-fashioned way. Find an artisan in your area and interview him or her in person or by telephone or letter. Explain to the class the artisan's views on his or her product.] One of the easiest ways for students to identify local artisans is to peruse back issues of local newspapers for feature articles. Other students might like to check hobby magazines and directories of organizations; these sources could provide lists of local affiliates. For example, if a student were interested in knives, a letter to Frank Centofante, The Knifemakers Guild, P.O. Box 928, Madisonville, TN 37554, or a look through an issue of *Blade* magazine could provide the name and address of one of the hundreds of men and women who craft knives by hand. What is typical of this product is generally typical of others: handmade items offer a beauty and quality not usually found in mass-produced items, but at much higher prices. There is also a

wide variation in quality, design, and materials.

Evaluation: [Decide whether Slater's construction of a spinning jenny was ethical in light of England's industrial secrets law. With your classmates, stage a mock trial and present your views.] Responses will vary. Students should have clearly defined reasons for the stance they take.

CONNECTING TO LITERATURE

Students might find Katherine Paterson's *Lyddie* to be informative and entertaining. Teachers seeking additional information might want to obtain Discovery Enterprise's collection of essays, *The Lowell Mill Girls: Life in the Factory.* Inquiries should be sent to Discovery at 134 Middle St., Lowell, MA 01852.

Immigration

Purpose

As a result of completing the activities on this Bloom sheet, the students will demonstrate growth in the following areas:

1. naming countries people emigrated from between 1890 and 1920;

2. relating information about Ellis Island and the Statue of Liberty;

3. explaining why various cultural groups immigrated in the past and why they wish to immigrate now; and

4. speculating on differences that might have resulted had another point of view prevailed.

Knowledge: [Prior to 1890, most U.S. immigrants came from northern and western Europe, especially England, France, and Spain. List the countries from which most immigrants came between 1890 and 1925.] Prior to 1890, most immigrants were from England, Spain, and France. After 1890 most immigrants came from the southern and eastern parts of Europe: Italy, Russia, Poland, Greece, Austria-Hungary, and Turkey. Many also came from Japan and other parts of Asia.

Comprehension: [Give three reasons why people wanted to emigrate.] Answers will vary but might include religious freedom, job opportunities, and freedom from political oppression.

Application: [Locate information about either Ellis Island or the Statue of Liberty. Summarize your findings and be prepared to share with the class.] Information should be available from numerous sources, including most encyclopedias.

Students might be interested to learn that the base on which the Statue of Liberty rests was paid for not with tax dollars, but with donations from the American public. The fund-raising drive was spearheaded by Joseph Pulitzer of the New York *World*. Money came from school children and their families in a grass-roots effort, not from private philanthropists. Pulitzer's name is inscribed on the base.

When the Statue of Liberty was "unveiled" (she had a drape across her eyes) on October 28, 1886, there was a gala celebration that included many orations. One of the most noteworthy remarks was made by the French engineer and promoter Ferdinand de Lesseps: "In landing beneath its rays, people will know they have reached a land where individual initiative is developed in all its power; where progress is a religion . . . ."

Further exploration might include discussion of the Emma Lazarus poem inscribed on the base of the Statue.

You will want to decide in advance how students can best present their information so that all students become familiar with both topics.

Analysis: [Predict the consequences if there were no limits set on immigration.] Answers may vary but are likely to include more competition for living space and fewer jobs.

Analysis: [Point out the advantages and disadvantages of having been a newcomer to the United States. Are these advantages and disadvantages different today than they were at the turn of the century? Support your answer.] Disadvantages might include limited knowledge of English, different customs, different styles of clothing, and limited job opportunities. Advantages might include religious freedom and economic opportunity.

Synthesis: [Suppose you are a newcomer to America. Write a report in journal form outlining your travels. Be sure to include difficulties experienced.] Answers will vary.

Evaluation: [Do you think our nation was built by immigrants and their descendants? Explain.] Although there would appear to be an obvious answer here, you may want to point out to students that we cannot overlook or undervalue the contributions of native Americans and of those who did not technically immigrate: slaves, indentured servants, and criminals.

Significant to our nation's development, too, was the support of other governments, especially Great Britain, France, Spain, and Russia.

EXTENDING THE STUDY

Have students investigate changes in attitudes toward groups of immigrants, from the welcome the Orientals received when the railroads were being built to the exclusionary policies implemented during World War II, for example. Discuss the reasons for the initial attitudes and for the changes in attitude. Were all Orientals treated the same? What other groups have had their immigration met with suspicion, distrust, and hostility? What groups have been universally welcomed? What accounts for the difference?

CONNECTING TO MUSIC

Secure examples of music from other cultures. Combine them with some contemporary selections such as "We Are the World" or the score from Neil Diamond's "The Jazz Singer."

CONNECTING TO GEOGRAPHY

Develop map skills by having students locate the countries listed in the knowledge task.

CONNECTING TO MATH AND SOCIOLOGY

Explore population trends and graph the results.

CONNECTING TO LANGUAGE ARTS

Numerous children's books deal with immigration. These are generally short enough to read and discuss in just a few minutes, and they are a wonderful source of information on diversity in custom, dress, and so on. Many also have enchanting artwork. If you can secure enough copies for students to explore these on their own, they may find that they are drawn to ones that deal with their own heritage. This in turn could lead to a sound oral history project for interested students: interview members of your family to discover what brought them to America.

Other short literary works that appeal to transescent students include the following:

Chief Seattle, "Letter to the U. S. Government"

Sandra Cisneros, "Eleven"

Ernesto Galarza, "Barrio Boy"

Francisco Jimenez, "The Circuit"

Myron Levoy, "Aaron's Gift"

Arthur Miller, "Grandpa and the Statue"

Lensey Namioka, "The All-American Slurp"

William Saroyan, "The Hummingbird That Lived Through the Winter"

Amy Tan, "Two Kinds" from *The Joy Luck Club*

Jade Snow Wong, "A Time of Beginnings"

"From Many Shores" by Barbara Elleman (*Book Links*, July 1993, p. 11) has an excellent annotated bibliography and many suggested activities involving books.

Yellow Journalism

Purpose

As a result of completing the activities on this Bloom sheet, the students will demonstrate growth in the following areas:

1. identifying major nineteenth-century journalists and listing their contributions;

1. demonstrating an understanding of exaggeration and unsupported facts in a news story; and

1. drawing and defending a conclusion about the power of the media to influence events.

Knowledge: [Define yellow journalism.] Yellow journalism is sensational writing that uses exciting but exaggerated contrivances (stories, photos, language, and/or headlines) to capture reader attention or to make a newspaper more popular. One of the more infamous headlines appeared in Pulitzer's New York *World* atop a story about 392 children who died in a heat wave: "How Babies Are Baked."

Comprehension: [Explain the relationship to yellow journalism of each of the following:]

Joseph Pulitzer was the owner of the New York *World* and a proponent of sensationalism in journalism. Ironically, Pulitzer later established a series of awards honoring all the best in American writing, as well as in other fields. The prize series is administered by Columbia University and was first awarded in 1917.

The New York *World* was newspaper home of such reporters as Stephen Crane, George Rhea, and Sylvester Scovel. The paper's editorial stance was that the United States had a responsibility to help Cuba throw off the yoke of Spanish colonialism. The paper's introduction of comics and subsequent feud with the New York *Journal* helped popularize U.S. involvement in Cuban affairs and is often credited with starting the Spanish-American war.

William Randolph Hearst was the owner of the New York *Journal*. Hearst sent Davis and Remington to Cuba to cover the rebellion against the Spanish colonial government. Legend has it that when Davis told Hearst there was no war to cover, Hearst cabled back that Davis should concentrate on the coverage—Hearst would *provide* the war. (Another version says it was Remington who objected and was told to provide pictures. No proof exists that the cable was real.) Hearst's feud with Pulitzer was fueled in part by Hearst's luring away

Pulitzer's entire Sunday magazine staff (except for one secretary.) His desire to steal "Hogan's Alley" was tempered by the *Journal*'s inability to publish in color. In anticipation of his acquisition of a color press, Hearst adopted the "Yeller Feller" as his mascot. He sponsored a Yeller Feller bicycle race from coast to coast. The San Francisco-to-New York relay took only thirteen days.

The New York *Journal* was Hearst's newspaper. The *Journal* reflected Hearst's belief that journalism was as much a matter of making the news as of recording it. The paper's early style and philosophy were precursors of today's investigative reporting. Like the *World*, the *Journal* touted its faith in science, in American ingenuity, and in progress. Though the paper prided itself on its "science" stories (often penned by Hearst himself) like those in today's tabloids, these stories often concerned themselves with two-headed calves, the world's fattest kid, or other sensational, pseudo-scientific subjects.

The Yellow Kid was a cartoon character who resided in Hogan's Alley and whose "bad boy" image allowed him to make derisive comments on the social structures of the day. The Yellow Kid was bald, snaggletoothed, and slightly Asian looking. His ears stood straight out from the sides of his head and his costume was an ankle-length dress that served as a billboard for a political lampoon, couched in dialect, camouflaged with humor, and changed daily. The yellow color—and hence the name—was accidental: a pressroom supervisor looking for a place to test a new smearproof yellow ink

painted the Kid's shapeless gown yellow. The Kid's outlandish clothing and puckish humor made him immediately popular with a wide audience.

"Hogan's Alley" was one of the first comics, though the idea of a serialized story told in strip form had not yet evolved. The Alley was peopled by a large number of slum-district ragamuffins who ridiculed upper-class fads. "Hogan's Alley" first appeared in the New York *World*. When it was lured away by the *Journal*, an imitation continued to appear in the *World*. A subsequent lawsuit over copyright spread the fame of "Yellow Kid Journalism" and increased the circulation of both papers to record numbers. The term was later shortened to "Yellow Journalism" and came to be applied to any sensationalistic news reporting.

Richard Felton Outcault was creator of "Hogan's Alley" and the Yellow Kid. Later he became even more famous for another of his cartoon characters, Buster Brown.

George Luks was the cartoonist who continued the Yellow Kid for the *World* when Outcault decamped for the *Journal*. Luks was chosen because he had already proved himself an able forger. An inveterate practical joker, Luks had frequently copied the work of his colleagues, adding some daring, controversial feature. He would surreptitiously slip the fakes onto the editor's desk, figuring that if one ever got by him and found its way into print, his colleague would get the blame!

Richard Harding Davis was a key figure in journalistic image-

making. Davis was a "celebrity reporter," both because of his social standing and because of his 1893 publication of the novella *Gallagher*. Davis was dispatched to Cuba by Hearst, who wanted Davis to report on the rebellion.

Frederic Remington was an American painter and sculptor who accompanied Davis to Cuba. His task was to provide sketches of the war. Though photography had been in use for more than half a century, newspapers had not yet mastered reproduction capability for photos.

The Spanish-American War, which lasted just over two months, was one of America's shortest wars. The last of many attempts to free Cuba from Spanish rule (the first revolt was in 1868), the war became America's war largely because of yellow journalism: stories recounted numerous atrocities and goaded American officials to act. Newspaper coverage of the sinking of the U.S. battleship *Maine* popularized the slogan "Remember the Maine!," which became a rallying cry leading to a declaration of war. America's benefits were both financial and political: the war protected America's sugar cane interests in Cuba, gave us access to new shipping channels in the Caribbean, and helped to establish our position as a Western power.

PUMP PRIMER

If your text has limited information on this topic and you want an alternative to lecturing or other teacher-dominated presentation, try employing a jigsaw cooperative learning method called Fact Phobia. Here's how it works.

1. Divide the class into six groups, making groups as nearly equal as possible. These groups are numbered and are called *base* groups.

2. Determine the largest number of students common to all groups and letter students accordingly. Thus, if every group has at least five students, but two groups have six, you'd assign the letter A, B, C, D, or E to one person in each group. The sixth person in the two over-sized base groups would be designated "wild."

3. The six base groups are research groups. They should be assigned two terms to research and become experts on. (If you include *yellow journalism*, you have twelve terms in all, or two per group.) Allow the groups time for media center research. Be sure to check with each of the base groups to verify the accuracy and completeness of their information.

4. Redivide the class into letter groups. Allow the wild cards to join a group of their choice. Each person is now to teach to the letter group the two terms researched in the base group.

5. Follow up with discussion or quiz to be sure that every student has mastered all twelve terms and is now cured of the "fact phobia."

This method of presentation has some distinct advantages over more traditional instruc-

tion. Students read a wide range of historical material while searching for their information. They truly become experts on their two terms when they know they have to teach them to their classmates. (This effect will increase dramatically with the second and subsequent opportunities to practice the technique.) And students seem to learn from each other better than they learn from adults.

Application: [Clip a news story from the daily paper and turn it into a piece of yellow journalism.] Answers will be varied. Yellow journalism stories shared some common traits: Headlines were exaggerated, satirical, or even frightening. They were usually large and frequently in color. Unsubstantiated opinion, if not easily disputed, was frequently stated as fact. Illustrations were usually dramatic or lurid. Facts, while not usually manufactured, were generally exaggerated to emphasize scandalous aspects of the story.

Application: [Collect information about another important journalist of this era and tell what contributions that person made to the changing face of journalism.] Among those students might investigate are Stephen Crane, George Rea, Sylvester Scovel, James Gordon Bennett, Charles A. Dana, Adolph Ochs, E. L. Godkin, William H. Hart, Ambrose Bierce, and Nellie Bly.

Crane, Rea, and Scovel were *World* reporters in the grand tradition of yellow journalism, though Crane's ultimate fame came in the area of fiction.

Bennett was owner of the New York *Herald*. He laid the foundation for common reporting by breaking the old taboos of language usage (using common terms and vulgarisms instead of genteel euphemisms) and of subject matter (he introduced "society" news, considered at first to be scandalous and gossipy).

Dana, owner of the New York *Sun*, was first to insist that stories have a human-interest angle.

Ochs, of the New York *Times*, called for a more mature, responsible press.

Godkin popularized the magazine *The Nation*.

Hart and Bierce worked for Hearst when he was with the San Francisco *Examiner*. Bierce later achieved fame as a short story writer, but is best remembered because of his mysterious disappearance.

Bly became famous for her exposés, researched at great danger to herself (e.g., she had herself committed to the asylum on Blackwell's Island so she could expose the plight of impoverished women there); she achieved even more fame once she began to travel with Buffalo Bill's Wild West Show.

Analysis: [Identify several common propaganda techniques, including bandwagon, name calling, card stacking, and transfer. Using newspapers, magazines, or advertising, provide an example of each. Tell how each might have been used by yellow journalists reporting on the Cuban rebellion.]

The bandwagon technique tries to persuade the reader to

follow a course of action because everybody else does. "The governor has support from all segments of society: agriculture, labor unions, business leaders, students and retirees alike. He represents you. Vote to reelect the people's governor."

Name-calling is using uses labels that evoke negative connotations, for example, "radical," "fascist," or "criminal."

Card stacking is telling only one side of a story. A writer with either a conservative or liberal bias often uses this approach.

Transfer is identifying an idea with a well-known idea, person, or event. For example, "Remember the Maine!" was reminiscent of "Remember the Alamo."

PUMP PRIMER —————

There are numerous other propaganda techniques that students may uncover. Some of the more prominent ones are these:

Glittering generalities: using vague phrases that promise much but don't mention how the promise will be carried out, for example, "The Great Society," "The New Deal," "Camelot."

Plain folks: convincing the reader that those in power are really no different than other people. A former Florida governor ran a "plain folks" campaign by taking periodic "work days": one month he might don a hard hat and work alongside a construction crew; the next might find him in a classroom, teaching; then he might join migrant workers picking crops.

Testimonial: using prominent people to endorse ideas or products. Arthur Ashe did some poignant endorsements for AIDS research just prior to his death.

Less frequently discussed techniques include nostalgia, brand loyalty, reward, humor, snob appeal, progress, image, scientific evidence, endorsement, authority, statistics, repetition, image maker, loaded words, and sex appeal.

Synthesis: [Design the front page of a newspaper in the style of yellow journalism.] Have students choose one event from the story of the struggle for Cuban independence and write a vivid, descriptive exaggeration of it. Have them try to cast suspicion on or put the blame on Spain.

This activity is more difficult than it sounds, even with the experience students gained while completing the first application activity. One reason is that the number of articles has increased. A second is that it is more difficult to change textbook language to a news format that to slant an existing news story. One way to make it easier is to allow students to work in pairs or small groups.

One issue that may have to be dealt with is the students' paradigms concerning *truth.* Some students believe that history and history texts are true: "they" couldn't print "it" if it weren't. They may object to taking something true and falsifying it or even slanting it.

You may want to deal with this issue head-on: students need to be aware that just

because a thing is in print, it isn't necessarily true. They need to become critical consumers not only of newspapers, but of magazines, textbooks, and other print materials. Or, you may skirt the issue by providing an alternate assignment. You might have some stories from newspapers or magazines (or carefully screened stories from tabloids) clipped and mounted on cardboard or construction paper. Allow students to scan one or more of these articles and record examples of yellow journalism.

PUMP PRIMER —————

Because the level at which transescent students are capable of abstract thought varies so greatly, you might want to conduct this activity in stages, using one type of read-around group (RAG). Here's how it works:

Students are given a specific amount of time to write a rough draft. This can be as little as fifteen minutes of class time or it can be an overnight homework assignment or a week-long project. It can be formatted as completely as you choose, from lists of ideas to full paragraphs.

Students are then divided into groups. Students take turns reading papers aloud to the small group. The reader is in charge of the discussion until satisfied with the outcome, at which point a new reader takes over.

You may want to provide some written suggestions for guiding the discussion. You might follow this format, providing a copy for each group:

Discussion Guide

1. What I liked about my paper was . . .

2. An area where I feel I need help is . . .

3. What strengths do you see in my paper?

4. What changes or additions would you suggest?

The rules are simple:

- The reader/writer retains complete control of the paper and is free to accept or reject all suggestions.

- Only positive comments and suggestions may be made.

- If you hear what you think is a good idea in someone else's paper, you may add it to your own.

- If you hear something with which you disagree, you may make a note to argue the point in your own paper: you may *not* disagree in the RAGs.

If time permits, shuffle the groups and repeat the process. This is especially advisable if students have never before used the technique. Some teachers prefer to do the two sessions on separate days, knowing that highly motivated students will revise between sessions. Other teachers move straight into the second set of RAGs from the first.

After the RAGs are completed, students are ready to do their final rewrite or to revise and peer edit, depending on the writing process you employ.

Evaluation: [Weigh what you see as the power of newspapers to influence events during the Spanish-American War against what you see as the power of today's media to influence world events. Make a case for or against the need for legislation requiring responsible, ethical journalism.] Answers will vary.

Evaluation: [Theodore Roosevelt referred to the Spanish-American War as "a splendid little war." Give reasons why many Americans in 1898 would have agreed with him.] Answers will vary, but should include references to yellow journalism.

CONNECTING TO SCIENCE

Investigate inks. What makes an ink smearproof? Why were some colors of ink more difficult to make smearproof than others?

CONNECTING TO GRAPHICS

Investigate how cartoons are printed. What difficulties are encountered when printing in color? Look at the same cartoon in several newspapers. What discrepancies in color exist?

CONNECTING TO LANGUAGE ARTS

Locate as many examples of Yellow Kid cartoons as possible. Analyze the humor: what is being ridiculed? What kind of language is used? What is difficult for you to understand or to find funny? Compare this humor with that found in such modern publications as *Mad* magazine or *National Lampoon.*

Students should discover that both lampoon current social issues, not necessarily relative to or funny during another time; both use current colloquial language; and both are examples of low humor, meant to be understood by the common man, though their creation required an informed, insightful intellect.

When looking at the cartoons and at the dialect, some students may be offended by what they see as racial slurs. You can defuse this issue by helping them to understand that these cartoons were not about racial distinctions, they were about social distinctions. The Yellow Kid was called that, not because of his faintly Asian appearance, but because of the yellow color of his dress. The dialect was not a racial dialect, but was a representation of the colloquial speech of the uneducated children throughout the tenements, regardless of ethnic origin. Point out, too, that in the New York of 1896 there was a preponderance of people who were recent immigrants or were first- or second-generation Americans. Many of them still exhibited a strong nationalism and were perhaps not as sensitive to ethnic references as we are today.

ADDITIONAL RESOURCES

Linderman, Gerald F. *The Mirror of War: American Society and the Spanish-American War.* University of Michigan Press, 1974.

Milton, Joyce. *The Yellow Kids: Foreign Correspondents in the Heyday of Yellow Journalism.* New York: Harper & Row, 1989.

The Annexation of Hawaii

Purpose

As a result of completing the activities on this Bloom sheet, the students will demonstrate growth in the following areas:

1. identifying and applying appropriate time concepts;

2. demonstrating a knowledge of place and location by creating a map;

3. relating economic and political conditions to historical change;

4. using a graphic organizer to summarize information; and

5. identifying the appropriate sources to obtain information using print materials and technology.

Knowledge: [Arrange the following in chronological order:]

1820 Missionaries arrive in Hawaii

1867 Midway Islands are annexed

1891 Queen Liliuokalani gives greater power to native Hawaiians

1893 American residents in Hawaii revolt

1898 Territorial status is granted to Hawaii

1959 Hawaii becomes the fiftieth state

Comprehension: [Explain why Hawaii was referred to as the "crossroads of the Pacific." Make a map of Hawaii to demonstrate your response.] The Sandwich (Hawaiian) Islands are located in a position ideal for trade. The islands were already regarded as an important port by traders stopping there en route to Asia. They also have been considered important as a military outpost. This feature has been responsible for the great mixture of ethnic groups within Hawaii.

Application: [Investigate what people in the 1800s believed were the pros and cons of annexing Hawaii. Organize your findings in a chart.] Answers will vary. Pros include the following: The location of the islands was good for trade; there was a fear that if the islands were not annexed by the United States, then Japan or another nation might assume control; and Americans viewed it as their responsibility to bring Christianity to native Hawaiians. Cons include the following: Annexation might lead to the formation of a colonial army; there was a fear of mixing another foreign population into the United States; and there was concern over ruling an area that, at the time, was not a candidate for statehood.

Analysis: [Determine the effects of the McKinley Tariff Act of 1890 on Hawaii.] The McKinley Tariff of 1890 ended the special status of Hawaiian sugar. As a result, the production of sugar dropped. This led to a rise in unemployment and to a decrease in property values.

Synthesis: [Suppose the United States had been unsuccessful in annexing Hawaii. How would this have affected trade?] Answers will vary.

Evaluation: [Criticize the actions of the American residents of Hawaii in 1893. Was the role they played in the revolt against the queen justified? Explain.] Answers will vary. In class discussion point out to students that in 1891, Queen Liliuokalani restored power to native Hawaiians. The Americans living in Hawaii did not like this. They revolted and asked the United States for help.

Soon after taking office, Grover Cleveland sent a representative to investigate the cause of the rebellion. The investigation revealed America's role in the rebellion. Grover Cleveland wanted the queen restored to power. This did not happen; instead, the Republic of Hawaii was established.

World War I

Purpose

As a result of completing the activities on this Bloom sheet, the students will demonstrate growth in the following areas:

1. explaining the impact of an individual on historical change;

2. perceiving events and issues as they were experienced by people at that time to develop historic empathy as opposed to present-mindedness; and

3. relating economic and political conditions to historical change.

Knowledge: [Describe the terrorist activity in Sarajevo that is generally thought to have precipitated World War I.] Key concepts that will assist students in understanding how one event can start a chain reaction leading to global warfare are *imperialism, nationalism,* and *militarism.* As European nations embraced these concepts, a spirit of suspicion and hostility began to build among nations.

Thus, although the assassination of Archduke Franz Ferdinand and his wife was planned and executed by a small group of Serbian patriots, Austria-Hungary did not go after the man who did the killing or even after the seven members of the secret society who were part of the conspiracy. Instead they presented a series of demands to the nation. When Serbia rejected several of the demands, Austria-Hungary declared war. Over the next four years, other nations joined in alliance with one nation or the other, until virtually the entire world was involved.

Comprehension: [Color a map of Europe to indicate which nations were part of the Central powers, which were part of the Allied powers, and which were neutral.] Most social studies texts or encyclopedias will provide a model and a check.

Application: [Write an editorial that might have appeared after the sinking of the Lusitania. In it, urge the United States to join or stay out of the Great War.] Answers will vary.

Analysis: [Make a poster showing how World War I was good

for certain groups in America.] Products will vary. Students should be aware that women began to experience new roles as workers in defense, construction, electronics, and other fields formerly closed to them. African Americans and other minorities also had more jobs open to them both in and out of the military, elevating both their image and their standard of living. The military profited from the passage of the Selective Service Act and the increased funding for shipping. Although economic conditions always relate somehow to historical change, students should be aware that war historically has stimulated American economy.

Synthesis: [Design a recruitment poster that might be used effectively to encourage war efforts today.] Products will vary. Students need to consider appeals to modern society and to consider propaganda techniques.

Evaluation: [Rank President Wilson's Fourteen Points in order of importance to America. Give a rationale for your order.] Answers will vary.

CONNECTING TO MUSIC

Have students study the effects of music on the patriotic mood of Americans. Among the songs they might consider are "The Caissons Go Rolling Along," "Keep the Home Fires Burning," "Over There," and "The Marine Hymn."

EXTENDING THE LESSON

Students might want to investigate airplanes and their function during the war (reconnaissance and bombing).

Students might discuss the importance of the Zimmerman message. Why did Germany want Mexico as an ally? How did the plan backfire?

The Roaring Twenties

Purpose

As a result of completing the activities on this Bloom sheet, the students will demonstrate growth in the following areas:

1. demonstrating an understanding of the time period in history known as the Roaring Twenties;

2. evaluating the pros and cons of buying items on credit;

3. relating economic and political conditions to historical change; and

4. personal involvement in developing a sociological representation of a decade.

Knowledge: [Name the president who held office from August 3, 1923, to March 4, 1929.] Calvin Coolidge.

Knowledge: [Describe the "good times" of the 1920s.] During the 1920s, people felt that life was good, and they wished to enjoy life to the fullest. People bought and sold stocks in an effort to "get rich quick." Jobs were plentiful, especially for those who lived in the city. The radio and electrical appliance industries were expanding, and the airplane and automobile were introduced at this time. Money was spent eagerly, but large debts resulted.

Comprehension: [Explain why the decade 1920–1929 was called "The Roaring Twenties."] The 1920s were considered "The Roaring Twenties" because of an overall feeling of prosperity and the carefree lifestyle that resulted. Despite a rise in organized crime, there was a burgeoning entertainment market, especially in the areas of radio and movies. Bathtub gin, bootleg whiskey, and speakeasies contributed to the party atmosphere.

PUMP PRIMER ————————

Students may wish to investigate organized crime during this time period. Moonshining and smuggling became big business since most people violated the Volstead Act (National Prohibition Act). Students might research Al Capone ("Scarface") and the St. Valentine's Day Massacre of 1929.

Application: [Find reasons why the United States was so prosperous during the 1920s.] The United States was not damaged by war as the European countries had been. The U.S. had a wealth of raw materials such as lumber and ore. Factories that had supplied the military during the war changed to the production of other needed items. The assembly line was introduced.

Analysis: [Explain the risks associated with buying items on credit.] When items are bought on credit, there is usually a small down payment and a promise to pay the rest later. People tend to "buy" more than they can afford, and a large debt can result.

PUMP PRIMER ————————

The class could debate buying items on credit versus paying cash, and this could be a tie-in to math and consumer skills. You might like to invite a consumer credit counselor to be a guest speaker.

Synthesis: [Originate a slogan that represents life in the 1920s. Display your slogan on a banner or poster.] Answers will vary.

Evaluation: [Prepare a logical argument for or against Prohibition.] Answers will vary. You may wish to point out that the Twenty-First Amendment repealed the Eighteenth Amendment in 1933. Encourage discussion about today's attitudes toward alcohol. Connect this to a drug and alcohol abuse presentation, perhaps in conjunction with a science teacher, a guidance counselor, or speakers from the community.

CONNECTING TO MUSIC

The music and dance crazes of the Flapper era are fascinating to some students. If you decide to explore this, be sure to include styles originated by African Americans such as jazz and the blues.

The Great Depression

Purpose

As a result of completing the activities on this Bloom sheet, the students will demonstrate growth in the following areas:

1. sensitivity to the plight of those who are victimized by

circumstances beyond their control;

2. personal involvement in developing a sociological representation of a decade;

3. questioning and hypothesizing about heroes; and

4. relating economic and political conditions to historical change.

Knowledge: [Create an artifact kit about the Great Depression. Work with classmates to set up a display for the school to see.] Responses will vary. This is a good project for whole class involvement or for small group work. More capable students may do well working alone. At a minimum, students should include a time line, a map of important locations, and photocopies of five or more photographs. Consider adding recipes, copies of music from the Thirties, copies of ads or price lists, letters, clothing—whatever is actually available or can be recreated from books.

PUMP PRIMER ————————

Artifact kits are available commercially from Jackdaw Publications, Division of Golden Old Publications, P.O. Box A03, Amawalk, NY 10501, and are discussed in detail in "History in My Hand: Making Artifact Kits in the Intermediate Grades" by Barbara A. Hatcher (*The Social Studies*, Nov./Dec. 1992, pp. 267–271).

Comprehension: [Chart the alphabet agencies of the Depression era. Give the name of the agency, the date it was established, its purpose, and its resolution (whether it still exists, whether it merged with another agency, and so on).] Answers will vary. Some of the following data may be included.

AAA (Agricultural Adjustment Agency): established in May 1933 to provide farm aid.

CCC (Civilian Conservation Corps): established in March 1933 to create jobs for unemployed youths. Most jobs involved reforestation or other ecology-related tasks. The CCC was dissolved after nine years.

FCA (Farm Credit Administration): established in June 1933 to refinance farm mortgages.

FDIC (Federal Deposit Insurance Corporation): established in 1933 to insure individual bank deposits and prevent bank failures, this agency still exists.

FERA (Federal Emergency Relief Administration): established in March 1933 to provide money to states for the unemployed.

FHA (Federal Housing Administration): established in 1934 to insure construction loans for housing.

HOLC (Home Owners Loan Corporation): established in June 1933 to offer mortgages to people who had lost their homes.

NRA (National Recovery Administration), established in June 1933 to provide business aid by controlling wages and working hours, both of which contributed to price controls.

PWA (Public Works Administration): established in 1933 to finance public projects such as dams and buildings.

SEC (Securities and Exchange Commission): established in 1934 to license stock exchanges and prevent market crashes. The SEC still exists.

TVA (Tennessee Valley Authority): established in May 1933 to buy, build, and operate dams along the Tennessee River.

WPA (Works Progress Administration): established in 1933 to provide jobs by constructing public buildings and by employing artists, actors, writers, and musicians to create works of art, write local histories, produce entertainment, and so on.

PUMP PRIMER ———————

Students should soon see that most of this legislation was accomplished in a short time—in fact, it was finished during the one hundred-day special session called by FDR shortly after his inauguration.

More capable students may want to explore whether there have been other presidents who have been able to goad Congress into such quick action, and what issues were involved.

Application: [Despite both the Depression and the Dustbowl in the Southwest, there were some enjoyable activities: the movies, the comics, the Big Bands, and radio's Golden Era. Illustrate one such aspect of life in the Thirties.] Products will vary.

Analysis: [Contrast the effects of the Depression on various segments of society, for example, city business owners, labor workers, southern tenant farm-

ers, Oklahoma sharecroppers, and California migrant workers.] Responses will vary.

Synthesis: [Hoover's response to the Depression was inadequate at best, and he was widely criticized for his refusal to establish direct federal aid. Yet Roosevelt's establishment of a national program has been condemned by those who say government aid destroys initiative and promotes helplessness. Working with one or two other students, generate a list of other solutions that might have been tried.] Responses will vary.

PUMP PRIMER ———————

Hoover took much of the blame for the Depression. Students might like to discover the meaning of such terms as "Hoover Hotels," "Hoover Flags," "Hoovervilles," and "Hoover Blankets." A typical dichotomy can be seen in Hoover's and Roosevelt's responses to the Bonus Expeditionary Forces (BEFs) of 1932 and 1933.

Evaluation: [Americans had no lack of heroes during this era. Speculate on why hard times would produce so many heroes. Decide which kind of hero would have had the most influence on you. Give at least three reasons for your choice.] Answers will vary. If students have difficulty identifying heroes, you might want to make available a list like the following one:

- the consummate politician Franklin D. Roosevelt, the first handicapped president, and his wife Eleanor

- gangsters such as Bonnie and Clyde, Pretty Boy Floyd,

Ma Barker, and John
Dillinger

- lawmen like J. Edgar Hoover
and Eliot Ness

- movie stars ranging from
Shirley Temple to Alice Faye,
from Mickey Mouse to Clark
Gable

- comic book heroes like Dick
Tracy, Buck Rogers, Tarzan,
and Little Orphan Annie

- socialites like Betty Hutton,
Alfred Vanderbilt, and
Brenda Frazier

- sports figures like Babe
Ruth and Shoeless Joe Jackson

- musicians like Duke Ellington, Louis Armstrong, and
Tommy Dorsey

PUMP PRIMER

Looking at heroes of the era
will almost certainly lead
students to discover some of the
racial inequities that existed
during this time frame. Open
discussion of topics like the
Negro baseball league or segregated hotel facilities may help
students understand that inequity is an ongoing, complex
problem that doesn't have a
simple solution. One of the classic ironies is that someone like
Louis Armstrong could play his
music in a restaurant that would
not seat him at its tables or serve
him food.

Students may also have difficulty with the fact that a gangster
or a person involved in scandal
could still be a hero. Allow them
to speculate on the causes. Be
sure they understand the
concept of the underdog and its
application to almost everyone

who was able to resist an unpopular government. Also, students
need to know that timing is
important—some of these
people were heroes at first, only
to "fall" in the public's estimation after some particularly
unheroic act. Have students
look for more modern examples
of questionable and fallen
heroes. Additionally, students
could use this discussion to
connect to a study of Robin
Hood.

EXTENDING THE STUDY:

One summary of the Great
Depression was that it taught
people to "use it up, wear it out,
make it do, or do without."
However, post-World War II prosperity combined with rapidly
changing technology to cause us
to abandon this philosophy and
become the "throw-away generation," manufacturing products
with "planned obsolescence" and
filling our landfills with plastics
and non-biodegradable materials. Have students speculate on
what life would be like today had
the economic sanctions of the
1930s become the norm, existing
even today.

World War II

Purpose

As a result of completing the
activities on this Bloom sheet,
the students will demonstrate
growth in the following areas:

1. identifying world leaders;

2. investigating experiences of
people who served during
World War II;

3. describing the impact of
human actions and natural
processes on the global environment;

4. explaining the effects of
major belief systems on
historical patterns of development;

5. identifying the importance
of technology as a catalyst for
change; and

6. explaining the impact of an
individual on historical
development.

Knowledge: [Tell the major
role played by each of these men
in World War II: Joseph Stalin,
Winston Churchill, Benito
Mussolini, Adolf Hitler,
Emperor Hirohito, Franklin D.
Roosevelt, and Harry S.
Truman.] Stalin was head of the
Communist party and ruler of
the Soviet Union. Mussolini was
the ruler of Italy. Churchill was
the prime minister of Great Britain. Hitler was the ruler of
Germany. Hirohito was the
emperor of Japan. Roosevelt
served three terms as U.S. president (1933–1945). Truman was
Roosevelt's vice president; he
became president after FDR's
death.

PUMP PRIMER

You may wish to have
students select one of the world
leaders and write a report. Information might include family
background, educational data,
and highlights of the subject's
political career.

Comprehension: [Give examples of ways in which women
helped the war effort.] Women
began working in many areas of

business and industry as well as in the professional fields, replacing the men who were called to serve. Women also served in the army (as WACs), navy (as WAVEs), the coast guard (as SPARs), and the Marine Corps. Women also played an important role as nurses, both at home and abroad.

PUMP PRIMER

Students might wish to investigate the changes in women's societal roles that were instigated during this era and actualized over the succeeding decades.

Some students might like to investigate the publicity given during wartime to changing women's roles through the use of such characters as Rosie the Riveter.

Application: [Interview a family friend or relative who served during World War II. If possible, examine photographs taken during that time period. Prepare a written report of your meeting.] Answers will vary. Contact local veterans' groups and request a guest speaker. The report may be assigned as a follow-up to the speaker's visit.

Analysis: [Survey members of your class to see if they agree or disagree with the use of the atomic bomb on August 6, 1945. Graph the results using a bar graph or a circle graph.] Answers will vary. Depending on the ability level of the students, you may need to give reminders regarding percents when working with the circle graph. This would be an opportunity to work with a math teacher on an interdiscipli-

nary activity, if you are assigned to teams.

Synthesis: [Choose one: compose a poem regarding World War II, create a poster to encourage people to enlist in the armed forces, or write a letter to the folks at home from a soldier in the war.] Answers will vary.

Evaluation: [Consider the results of your survey from the analysis activity. What recommendation would you have made to the president regarding the bombing of Japan? What arguments would you present to support your recommendation?] Answers will vary.

CONNECTING TO LITERATURE

Some students might like to read *The Cay* by Theodore Thomas. (Students from landlocked areas will usually pronounce *cay* as [kā] to rhyme with *pay*, but it is more generally pronounced [kē] to rhyme with *sea*. There are several other spellings of [kē], *key* and *quay* being the most common.)

The United Nations

Purpose

As a result of completing the activities on this Bloom sheet, the students will demonstrate growth in the following areas:

1. analyzing the causes and consequences of, and possible solutions to, persisting contemporary issues and emerging global issues;

2. evaluating the role of international and multinational organizations in global affairs;

3. explaining the impact of individuals, events, and trends on historical development;

4. describing the impact of human actions and natural processes on the global environment;

5. identifying likenesses and differences in dissimilar data; and

6. oral skills.

Knowledge: [Describe the reason for creating the United Nations.] Franklin D. Roosevelt believed that the nations of the world should join together to form an organization whose main purpose was to try to keep world peace and guarantee the Four Freedoms to all individuals.

Knowledge: [List the six branches of the United Nations.]

General Assembly
Security Council
Secretariat
International Court of Justice
Economic and Social Council
Trusteeship Council

Comprehension: [Describe the role of each branch of the United Nations.] Answers are available in encyclopedias and textbooks.

Application: Draw a chart or diagram that shows the six branches of the United Nations.] Work will vary.

Analysis: [Determine how FDR's Four Freedoms and Woodrow Wilson's Fourteen Points influenced the United Nations. Write a report stating your findings.] Woodrow Wilson listed fourteen points that he felt should be the basis for a peace agreement in 1918. His list included a recommendation for the formation of an organization made up of major countries whose purpose would be to prevent a future war. This led to the formation of the League of Nations. The United States was not a member however. In 1941, FDR's Four Freedoms were included in the Atlantic Charter. Twenty-six nations signed this charter and were referred to as "the United Nations."

Synthesis: [Design a plan for world peace. Share your plan for peace through a skit, a poem, or a song. Be specific and include a set of rules and standards.] Work will vary.

Evaluation: [Decide if it is necessary to have United Nations peace-keeping forces. Justify your opinion with three reasons.] Responses will vary. Students may be interested in discussing the situation in areas of the world where UN peace-keeping forces are or have been involved.

ADDITIONAL TEACHER RESOURCES

America and Its People

Everyman's United Nations. New York: United Nations, 1964.

Communism

Purpose

As a result of completing the activities on this Bloom sheet, the students will demonstrate growth in the following areas:

1. investigating the ideology, institution, processes, and political culture of Communism;

2. explaining the effects of a major belief system on historical patterns of development;

3. constructing a time line;

4. oral skills;

5. perceiving events and issues as they were experienced by people at that time and developing historical empathy as opposed to present-mindedness; and

6. identifying the appropriate sources to obtain information using print materials and technology.

Knowledge: [Use a time line or flow chart to show, by nation, the spread of Communism from the Bolshevik Revolution in 1917 to the present. Color code your entries to distinguish those nations that are no longer Communist from those that still are Communist.] Answers will vary.

Comprehension: [Explain the three key Communist concepts of historical materialism, dialectical materialism, and economic determinism.]

Historical materialism divided society into two classes: the *bourgeoisie*, the elite class, and the *proletariat*, the workers. This division continued until the rich become so rich and the poor so poor that revolution occurred. Because this division was at the root of all human misery, it was the Communists' obligation to speed the process toward revolution.

Dialectical materialism held that nothing is permanent and the change process is cyclic: a combination of actions and events build up to a state called thesis; opposing forces, called the antithesis, overthrow the thesis; this sets up a new ruling state, called synthesis, which evolves into a new thesis. The Communist position was that Communist victory in these changes was inevitable (dialectic).

Economic determinism decreed that the individual was entirely a product of the economic system under which he or she grew. Since capitalism was a degenerate economic system, the Communist had an obligation to overthrow it so that the future of the world could be determined by the better system.

Application: [Work with others to produce a mural depicting life under Communism in the Soviet Union.] Work will vary.

Analysis: [Investigate one of the American socialist Utopian projects. In what ways was it similar to Marxist-Leninist Communism? How was it different?] Answers will vary. If students have difficulty locating references to such Utopian projects, suggest that they investigate one of these:

The Amana Society near Davenport, Iowa

The Rappites at Harmony, Indiana

The Owenites at New Harmony, Indiana

The Harmonists at Economy, Pennsylvania

The Separatists of Zoar, Ohio

The Shakers, Mount Lebanon, New York, and 17 other locations

John Humphrey Noyes' Oneida Community, New York

The Wallingford Perfectionists, Connecticut

The Aurora Commune in Oregon

The Bethel Commune in Missouri

The Icarians near Corning, Iowa

The Bishop Hill Colony, Henry County, Illinois

The Cedar Vale Commune, Howard County, Kansas

The Social Freedom Community, Chesterfield County, Virginia

The Anaheim Associates Cooperative, California

The Vineland Colony, New Jersey

Silkville Prairie Home Colony, Franklin County, Kansas

Brook Farm, West Roxbury, Massachusetts

Bronson Alcott's Fruitlands, Harvard, Massachusetts

Synthesis: [Produce a skit or role-play that presents one person's experience with the fall of the Berlin Wall or with the fall of Soviet Communism.] Products will vary.

Evaluation: [Attempts to achieve communal societies

have been as massive as Soviet Communism and as limited as the Cedar Vale Community, as apolitical and unstructured as Haight-Ashbury and as rigid and sectarian as Jonestown. List seven to ten reasons why most of these ventures have failed. Make another list of things you think are necessary for a society to survive.] Answers will vary.

The Korean Conflict

Purpose

As a result of completing the activities on this Bloom sheet, the students will demonstrate growth in the following areas:

1. comparing political systems and ideologies;

2. examining the creation and resolution of conflict among nations;

3. evaluating the role of international organizations in global affairs;

4. identifying the importance of technology as a catalyst for change; and

5. organizing information in a journalistic format.

Knowledge: [Create a historical marker commemorating an event during the Korean Conflict relative to one of the following:]

The United Nations. Organized in 1945, the United Nations is an alliance of the world's nations. Like the League of Nations (created after World War I), its purpose is to effect peaceful settlements of disputes

between nations. While all member nations are represented in the General Assembly, the Security Council, which has the power to investigate disputes and to order action against aggressor nations, has representatives from only five nations. Each of the "Big Five" Security Council members has the power to veto such actions. However, the Soviet Union was boycotting the Security Council when the Korean Conflict erupted, and so was unable to exercise its veto power. The subsequent defense of South Korea marked the first time the Communists had been stopped by forces mobilized on an international scale.

Harry S. Truman. President of the United States when Communist North Korea invaded South Korea, Truman's responses to the UN request for help was controversial: he sent U.S. troops into China as a "police action," without making a formal declaration of war. His inability to bring the "conflict" to a quick close and his removal of the popular general Douglas MacArthur were leading controversies during his presidency.

The Soviet Union. The bed of European Communism, the Soviet Union boycotted the UN Security Council because of its refusal to recognize the government of Communist China, with whom she had formed a defensive alliance. Though the Soviet Union supposedly had withdrawn her troops from the Democratic People's Republic of Korea (North Korea), she encouraged North Korea to unite Korea under Communist control by training and equipping North Korean troops.

Dwight D. Eisenhower.
One of the most popular heroes of World War II, Eisenhower was seen as a viable alternative to the problem of having a civilian in charge of the military: having an ex-military man in charge. Eisenhower promised a quick end to the Korean Conflict, and his "I Like Ike" campaign successfully reflected the national mood.

Red China. The People's Republic of China was established under the Communist forces led by Mao Tse-tung, who in 1949 successfully defeated the Nationalist government headed by Chiang Kai-shek by forcing Chiang Kai-shek to retreat to the island of Taiwan (Formosa). When UN forces approached the Yalu River, which separates North Korea from China, Red China openly began sending Chinese troops to the aid of the North Koreans.

Douglas MacArthur.
Appointed commander of the UN forces in Korea, MacArthur was considered a brilliant strategist. His forces landed at Inchon, behind the North Korean line that had been established near Pusan, causing the North Koreans to retreat and defend their homeland. MacArthur's push on into North Korea and his hawkish insistence on expanding the fighting by taking military action against China were factors in Truman's relieving him of his command, citing insubordination.

The Cold War. Following the devastation of World War II, the Soviet Union and the United States began a race to develop themselves as nuclear superpowers. Because each nation was unwilling virtually to assure its own destruction by firing on the other, the "cold war" that resulted was largely a lot of muscle flexing and posturing. One-upmanship became the order of the day as the U.S. first exploded a nuclear bomb, then the Soviet Union developed the bomb *and* launched the first successful missile-carrying satellite, *Sputnik I.* Since each nation was reluctant to engage the other directly in war, so the cold war became a contest of propaganda, economic pressure, and military threats.

Joseph Stalin. Leader of Communist Russia, Stalin attempted to expand Soviet influence throughout Asia. World domination, in fact, became the goal, leading Stalin's successor, Nikita Khrushchev, to announce to the United States, "We will bury you," a prediction that happily proved baseless. It was the internal strife that resulted from Stalin's death that weakened Soviet support of North Korea and facilitated peace talks.

The 38th Parallel. The closest geographic designation to the line of demarcation between North and South Korea. Once North Korea was able to repel UN forces behind the 38th parallel, it became the scene of most of the fighting until the end of the conflict. The armistice signed July 27, 1953, established a dividing line that crossed the 38th parallel.

Joseph McCarthy. A Republican senator from Wisconsin, McCarthy became a zealot in the cause of finding "communist sympathizers" and "subversives" in the largest episode of mass hysteria since the Salem Witchcraft Trials (to which McCarthyism was frequently compared). Using his position as chairman of the Government Operations Committee, McCarthy capitalized on the widespread fear of Communism during the cold war to bolster his own popularity. McCarthy's open, unfounded attack on the U.S. military led to his subsequent humiliation on national television and led the Senate to censure McCarthy for "conduct unbecoming a member." The mood that allowed McCarthyism to exist as long as it did also allowed one of the bloodiest wars in America's history to be undeclared except as a "police action."

PUMP PRIMER ――――――

As a way of presenting this material, you might find it convenient to divide the class into pairs or triads and to assign them topics for their markers. Thus, when the presentations are made to the class, all ten topics will have been covered, and you can fill in any missing information at that point.

PUMP PRIMER ――――――

Students might wish to compare McCarthyism with the "Red Scare" of the 1920s and to look at the cultural factors that allowed such ideologies to exist.

The role of technology in the Korean Conflict might also be investigated by students. Not only was the development of the hydrogen bomb an important factor in the arms race, but the advent of television meant that more Americans had direct access to public policy information. Nixon, who came to be called America's first media president because of his use of television to promote his own image, began his manipulation of television with his famed "Checkers Speech," offered during the Korean Conflict.

PUMP PRIMER

Since World War II, military service by presidential candidates has become more and more of a campaign issue. Students might wish to look in particular at how it became an issue in the election of Bill Clinton and to determine the extent of trickle down: during the Nineties, has military service been a factor in state and local campaigns as well? Students may be surprised to learn that not only is the issue of civilian control of the military not a closed issue, but that military service is a hot issue even in local elections and appointments, at least among some factions.

Comprehension: [Do a RAFT writing assignment that summarizes the Korean Conflict.] RAFT is an acronym for Role-Audience-Format-Topic. Nancy Vandervanter, a teacher-participant in the Montana Writing Project, is credited with its invention. Its use provides students with an organizational structure and a point of view, both of which are often missing in transescent writing. The use may be serious or fanciful. For example, the student may assume the persona of a U.S. soldier (role) writing a letter (format) to his girlfriend (audience) or of a South Korean reporter writing an article for a newspaper. Or, at the risk of

descending into the absurd, the student could write as the voice of a Soviet-made bullet dictating its own obituary for a Soviet newspaper before giving its life in the service of its country. Providing the students with some improbable RAFTs will stimulate creative approaches without blocking the intent of the activity. Remind students that in every case the topic has been dictated by the task and that summarizing the conflict is the primary focus.

Application: [Create a storyboard to retell the major events of the conflict. Include an interesting opening, six "cliffhangers" (for fade-to-commercials), and a satisfactory closure.] Products will vary.

Analysis: [Compare the isolationist policy of the United States after World War I to its policies after World War II, including the Marshall Plan, the Korean Conflict, and SEATO. Decide what caused this shift of focus. Present your ideas to the class.] Answers will vary. Students should probably see that development of electronic media was "shrinking" the world and isolationism was no longer in America's best interest, if in fact it ever had been. One thing that Pearl Harbor taught us was that the "ostrich approach" might keep us from seeing the evil around us, but it presented a very inviting target for our enemies' boots.

Synthesis: [Revise your RAFT writing, changing one major factor and predicting how that change would have affected the course of the conflict.] Responses will vary. If students need help deciding what to

change, try letting them brainstorm "what if's." Some possibilities: What if the United States had refused to enter an undeclared war? What if the Soviet Union had entered the dispute on the side of North Korea? What if MacArthur had been successful in invading China, despite Truman's orders? What if the Soviet Union had not been boycotting the Security Council meeting where the appeal for help was heard? What if Red China had developed nuclear capabilities at this point in time?

Evaluation: [Make a decision scale weighing the advantages and disadvantages of having a civilian (the president) in charge of the military. Put the pros on one side and the cons on the other. Decide as you go if some of the items should weigh more (be bigger) than others. Tilt the top of the scale to show if it balances in favor of the pros or the cons.] Responses will vary. Remind students that this is not the first time that this has been an issue: Scott's removal by President Polk during the Mexican War was a response to this same issue.

John F. Kennedy

Purpose

As a result of completing the activities on this Bloom sheet, the students will demonstrate growth in the following areas:

1. speculating on differences that might have resulted had another point of view prevailed;

2. explaining the impact of an individual on historical development; and

3. analyzing the various roles of a belief system as they relate to the individual.

Knowledge: [Assume the role of a biographer about to interview Kennedy in the summer of 1963. Because he is such a busy president, you will be allowed to ask only ten questions. Make a list of the questions you will ask and supply his probable answers.] Choices will vary. Students may need help with question-writing in order to avoid asking questions that are simplistic, rhetorical, or too open-ended. They will need to keep in mind that since they can ask only ten questions, probing follow-up questions may be a luxury they cannot afford. This is a good interdisciplinary link with teaching interview techniques in a journalism or language arts classroom.

Comprehension: [Kennedy was America's first Catholic president. Discuss why his religion was a campaign issue.] Students may find many different answers to this question, but one issue that should be mentioned is abortion. In the decade or so prior to the *Roe v. Wade* decision, abortion, like all feminist issues, was a hot political topic. Many people feared that with a practicing Catholic in the White House, abortion laws would never pass the Congress.

PUMP PRIMER ————

Students may be interested in discovering more about the issue of a president's personal religious beliefs, especially in light of the idea of separation of church and state. Personal beliefs were again a consideration in the election of a Quaker, Richard Nixon, during the Vietnam conflict, and with the election of a Southern Baptist, Jimmy Carter.

Application: [Make a record book listing the accomplishments and failures of Kennedy during his term of office. If possible, include quotes, pictures, and anecdotes.] Responses will vary.

Analysis: [One of the ways to tell what a person is like is to look at the person's heroes. Kennedy wrote about some of his heroes in a book called *Profiles in Courage*. Read one of the profiles and tell how Kennedy was like the person profiled. What challenge did the person meet? What was the result?] Responses will vary but should include the idea that each stood up for what he or she thought was right, regardless of personal cost. Students may be interested to learn the reason JFK wrote this book: he was recuperating from back surgery and couldn't tolerate the boredom of lying in bed.

PUMP PRIMER ————

Gabrielle Rico and Fran Claggett, in *Balancing the Hemispheres: Brain Research and the Teaching of Writing*, describe a type of graphic summarizer and organizer called a *Mandala*. Though traditional mandalas are in various Oriental religions symbols of the universe, mandalas have begun springing up in jewelry and art as symbols of anything cyclic or united. Typically their shape is circular, though balance and symmetry are sometimes achieved within other shapes.

Students should begin their mandala about JFK by filling out a worksheet comparing Kennedy and the person whose profile they studied (see below for a sample). Then they should draw a symbol to represent each cell. For example, on the sample page students might fill in the line "Color that describes" with "Red" and draw a bleeding heart as a symbol (symbolic of his wounds, of his courage in World War II, or of his being called a "bleeding heart Liberal" by some of his detractors); the students might decide to draw a black arrow as their own symbol, symbolizing an ability to deal swiftly and truthfully with issues. Next they write a statement summarizing each person—one sentence about Kennedy and one about the person profiled.

To construct the mandala, the students divide a circle in half, using a single straight line or a symbol of some sort. Symbols representing Kennedy are transferred to one semicircle and the sentence copied around its edge; the process is repeated on the other side for the profiled subject. The addition of color complete the art portion of the project. Encourage balance and symmetry in the design.

To complete the writing portion of the project, the students return to the adjectives listed and use them to write paragraphs (character sketches) about the subjects.

Synthesis: [Suppose that Kennedy had not died in Dallas.

Make a list of outcomes that might have resulted from his finishing his term of office.] Responses will vary. If time permits, students might want to investigate the assassination. Have them recreate crime reports and drawings. Hold a board of inquiry and reach a decision. Guest assistance might come from an investigator, a forensic scientist, or a criminologist. Assistance can be found in Eugene Baker's *At the Scene of the Crime* and *In the Detective Lab*, both from Child's World, 1980.

Evaluation: [Kennedy is generally credited with five major accomplishments: proposing significant civil rights legislation, establishing the Peace Corps, providing support for the manned space program, patronizing the fine arts, and supporting an atomic test ban. Of these five, which do you think was most important? Why?] Answers will vary. Require justification.

Mandala Worksheet

	JFK (name it)	Most like (describe it)	Most like (describe it)	Profile (name it)
Career				
Plant or animal most like				
Color that describes				
Music that describes				
Avocation				
Most courageous decision				
Element most like (air, fire, water, earth)				

Ideas in Bloom

The War in Vietnam

Purpose

As a result of completing the activities on this Bloom sheet, the students will demonstrate growth in the following areas:

1. recognizing that there are multiple possible interpretations of any historical event;

2. analyzing various interpretations of historical events and drawing conclusions from given information;

3. investigating how cause and effect relationships precipitate change;

4. perceiving events and issues as they were experienced by people at that time to develop historic empathy as opposed to present-mindedness; and

5. explaining the effects of a major belief system on historical development.

Knowledge: [Explain the Tonkin Gulf Resolution and how it differed from a congressional declaration of war.] The Tonkin Gulf Resolution was the result of Johnson's announcement that an American warship had been attacked by North Vietnamese gunboats. The resolution gave the president unlimited authority to use "all necessary means including the use of armed forces" to stop the aggressive acts. A formal declaration of war would have involved America's allies.

Comprehension: [Although the war in Vietnam had been going on for twenty years when Lyndon Johnson took office and America's policy on containment of Communism dated back to the Eisenhower administration in the late 1950s, Johnson took most of the blame for the war in Vietnam. Explain how the actions Johnson took caused him to be blamed.] The key to the blame was escalation. The war started as a civil war between factions in a country divided against itself over the issue of government once the French withdrew. Eisenhower, eager to contain the spread of Communism, sent "advisors" and military "aid." Kennedy increased the number of advisors from about 650 to over 16,000. But Johnson ordered American warplanes to bomb the country and sent hundreds of thousands of troops—it was estimated at the height of the war that there were more than 538,000 American soldiers in Vietnam *at the same time.* By the end of the war, America had dropped more bombs than she had used in all of World War II and Korea combined, had lost more than 55,000 lives, and had more than 300,000 wounded.

Application: [Write an editorial in which you take the position of a 1960s hawk or dove and express your opinion on American involvement in the Vietnam War.] Students should show an understanding that hawks believed that the war resulted from Communist aggression and that the U.S. had an interest in stopping the spread of Communism, while doves saw the war as an internal issue and felt that the U.S. should mind its own business.

PUMP PRIMER

The above definitions of *hawk* and *dove* are prime examples of oversimplification, but they will serve to guide the students. However, students might want to locate actual editorials and speeches from the Vietnam era and to classify their authors as hawks or doves. Such an examination would serve as a good prewriting activity for this task.

Analysis: [The Vietnam War was fought for the same principles that had precipitated the Korean Conflict, yet it met with little of the popular acceptance evident during the Korean Conflict. Make a chart or diagram that compares the two hostilities and try to account for the differences in perspective.] Answers will vary. Some key elements might include the following:

- America was war weary, having been involved in either war or cold war since 1940.

- The Korean Conflict was much shorter than the Vietnam War.

- The Vietnam War caused more loss of American life.

- The end of McCarthyism, the Bay of Pigs fiasco, and other such ignominies reduced fear of the "Red Threat."

- The rules of war changed with the advent of guerrilla warfare, chemical warfare, and sabotage.

- The rise of technology brought the fighting in Vietnam in to America's living room.

Synthesis: [Create a display featuring the counterculture that grew out of the disillusionment of youth with the dominant culture of the 1960s and its participation in the Vietnam War. Include clothing, hairstyles, music, language, art, fads, and so on in your display.] You may wish to turn this into a whole class project, making each student responsible for one or two items. You might want to procure a variety of written documents, oral history interviews, literature, artifacts, art, music, photos or replicas of historical monuments, other photographs, and historical film footage.

Evaluation: [Explain how America achieved (or did not achieve) "peace with honor" in Vietnam. Base your conclusions on your study of Vietnam.] Answers will vary.

CONNECTING TO LITERATURE

Students might enjoy reading about another teenager's attempts to make sense of the war by reading the fiction book *Park's Quest* by Katherine Peterson or *December Stillness* by Mary Downing Hahn.

The Green Berets

Purpose

As a result of completing the activities on this Bloom sheet, the students will demonstrate growth in the following areas:

1. investigating the values of a society by looking at its heroes;

2. examining the effects on society of individuals and their actions;

3. recognizing that there are various ways of viewing events; and

4. organizing information in a graphic format.

Knowledge: [Briefly tell how the U.S. Special Forces came into being.] In the early 1960s, President John F. Kennedy became convinced that the rules of warfare had irrevocably changed and that a new kind of fighting force had to be established. Often alone in his evaluation of the situation, Kennedy set about convincing first his military advisers and then the Congress that what was needed was, as he said in his commencement address at West Point in 1962, "a new and wholly different kind of military training." Drawing on the experiences of the OSS (the Office of Strategic Services, in existence from 1942-1945, and the first to encounter guerrilla warfare), the U.S. Army developed plans for training its Special Forces unit for guerrilla warfare and located its training site at Fort Bragg, North Carolina. The green beret is the hat worn by a Special Forces member, but the media capitalized upon its unusual nature to make the term synonymous with the man. Thus, following popular (but not military) usage, we shall use the terms "Green Berets" and "Special Forces" interchangeably.

Comprehension: [Explain how guerrilla warfare differs from combat.] Answers will vary but should indicate that guerrilla warfare includes the use of subversives, assassins, and infiltrators, the use of ambush instead of direct engagement, and the use of psychological warfare.

Application: [Make a "Mobile of Fame" having at least five shapes on which you have mounted facts about ten Green Berets.] Products will vary. Students may wish to make all five shapes identical or to vary them. Suggest that the shapes be symbolic. Specific profiles might be written about some of the following SF members, but students should be encouraged to include any local members who can be found and interviewed or any who were written up in local newspapers: Gen. William Yarborough, Col. Charles M. "Bill" Simpson, Col. Aaron Bank, Col. "Iron Mike" Paulick, Maj. William "Peanut" Hinton, Lt. Col. James N. "Nick" Rowe, Maj. Ralph "Pappy" Shelton, Capt. "Hairbreadth" Harry Cramer, Capt. Ron Shackleton, Maj. Larry Thorne, Maj. Jim Ruhlin, Maj. Ola Mize, Capt. "Bo" Gritz, Col. Francis Kelly, and Col. Charles "Charging Charlie" Beckwith. For biographical information, students might consult books about the Vietnam War and about the control of Communism in Latin America, back issues of news magazines, and *Current Biography.*

Analysis: [Although there were other irregular warfare forces established after World War II, the Green Berets achieved more recognition than other groups such as the navy's

SEAL teams or the air force's Air Commandos. Compare the work of these three special forces and draw a conclusion about why the Green Berets were so well known.] Answers will vary, but students should consider such factors as the unusual beret itself, the popular song by Sgt. Barry Sadler (one of the few to compliment some aspect of what was to be a most unpopular war), and the influence of writer Robin Moore and of Hollywood star John Wayne.

Synthesis: [Compose a song or poem expressing your feelings about some aspect of warfare or the military.] You may need to do a good deal of groundwork for this activity, as students may disagree sharply on the issue of having a military at all.

This is a good place to connect to music. Students should hear Barry Sadler's "The Ballad of the Green Beret," but they should also hear some of the protest songs of the sixties.

Encourage discussion about belief systems that object to war in general as well as belief systems that found this war in particular to be unacceptable. If time permits, allow students to search newspapers for stories, cartoons, and editorials to support their own viewpoint. Once the foundation has been laid, encourage students to compose their stories, songs, or poems and to share them with one another. Establish ground rules for dealing with controversy, allowing students to disagree without being disagreeable.

Evaluation: [The Green Berets' medical teams worked not only on curing falciprium malaria, tropical sprue, and other diseases that affected soldiers, but also on treating leprosy in and providing inoculations for civilians. Consider whether the good that they did outweighed their mortality rates and whether they were a necessary part of the war. Argue your conclusions in an editorial, giving support for your arguments.] Answers will vary.

The Civil Rights Movement

Purpose

As a result of completing the activities on this Bloom sheet, the students will demonstrate growth in the following areas

1. understanding that with rights also go responsibilities; and

2. understanding of our constitutional rights.

Knowledge: [Read the Bill of Rights. Select three of these amendments and list the rights they guarantee to all Americans.] Answers will vary. Students may need to work in cooperative learning groups to complete this activity. You could prepare copies of the Bill of Rights. Students could divide the reading and discuss the meanings of the amendments in groups.

Comprehension: [Explain what is meant by "separate but equal."] Answers will vary. It

should be pointed out to students that a Supreme Court decision in 1896 upheld a Louisiana law that required separate but equal accommodations for blacks and whites in railroad cars. This "separate but equal" rule was loosely interpreted for more than fifty years. Students could investigate and list some of the many applications of the "separate but equal" principle found in the South.

Application: [Learn the important dates in the civil rights movement and show them on a time line.] Dates can be found in encyclopedias as well as in textbooks.

Analysis: [Point out the significance to the civil rights movement of the Thirteenth Amendment, the Supreme Court decision in *Brown* v. *Board of Education of Topeka*, and the Civil Rights Act of 1964.] The Thirteenth Amendment abolished slavery in 1865. During the Reconstruction period, significant progress was made toward achieving equal rights. In 1954, the Supreme Court abolished segregation in public schools. The Civil Rights Act of 1964 is a law banning discrimination due to a person's color, race, religion, sex, or national origin.

Synthesis: [Working with a partner, make a list of five rights to which all people are entitled regardless of race or religion.] Answers will vary. Students might want to compare their lists with others' and with Roosevelt's "Four Freedoms."

Evaluation: [Rank your list of five rights, placing the most important one first. Justify your choices.] Answers will vary.

Evaluation: [You are responsible for developing a new code of conduct for your school. Determine the rights that should be guaranteed to all students.] Answers will vary.

CONNECTING TO LITERATURE

Students wishing to know more about the U.S. Constitution and its civil rights guarantees might enjoy reading Denis J. Hauptly's *A Convention of Delegates.*

Martin Luther King, Jr.

Purpose

As a result of completing the activities on this Bloom sheet, the students will demonstrate growth in the following areas:

1. writing a summary;

2. explaining the impact of an individual on historical development;

3. speculating on differences that might have resulted from another point of view;

4. perceiving events and issues as they were experienced by people at that time to develop historic empathy as opposed to present-mindedness;

5. identifying likenesses and differences in dissimilar data; and

6. using a graphic organizer to summarize information.

Knowledge: [Read a biography of Martin Luther King, Jr. Find pictures that represent at least ten significant events in his life. Organize them on a poster or collage or in a scrapbook.] Biographies of King abound, but one particularly readable one for middle schoolers is Edward Preston's *Martin Luther King: Fighter for Freedom* (Doubleday, 1970). Less able students may want to read a biographical sketch from an encyclopedia or biographical dictionary.

Another approach might be to take a biography and use the "Jigsaw" cooperative learning (or the Read a Book in an Hour) technique: the students could each read a chapter and report to the entire class. Students could also work in pairs or triads to complete the remainder of the activity.

Comprehension: [Locate and read the text of three of Martin Luther King's statements or speeches. Write a one-sentence summary of the main idea of each.] Suggested speeches: "I Have a Dream"; the Nobel Peace Prize acceptance speech; "The Drum Major Instinct"; "I've Been to the Mountaintop"; Letter from the Birmingham Jail."

Application: [Locate the lyrics of three to five songs important during the civil rights movement, including "We Shall Overcome." Explain their significance to the movement.] Suggested songs: "Lift Every Voice and Sing" by James Weldon Johnson; "Kumbaya"; "Oh Freedom" by Hall Johnson; "Let There Be Peace on Earth."

Analysis: [Compare King's "I Have a Dream" speech with Langston Hughes' poem "I Dream a World." How are they similar? How different? What other evidence can you find to show how black authors influenced King?] Answers will vary.

Synthesis: [Write a play, poem, or essay about overcoming prejudice.] Products will vary.

Evaluation: [Report on the contribution to the civil rights movement of another individual of your choice. Decide how that person influenced, or was influenced by, King. Justify your answer.] Answers will vary.

PUMP PRIMER

If students need a list from which to choose an individual, suggest these: Jackie Robinson, Mahalia Jackson, Rosa Parks, Marian Anderson, Mahatma Gandhi, John F. Kennedy, Malcolm X, Roy Wilkins, Lester Granger, A. Philip Randolph, Adam Clayton Powell, James Farmer, Kenneth B. and Mamie Clark, Ralph Abernathy, Coretta Scott King, Medgar Evers, Andrew Young, Jesse Jackson, Whitney Young, James Baldwin.

Students need to be aware that the civil rights movement will probably never end, as equity is an unachievable ideal. Its elusiveness does not diminish its importance or its urgency. Students also need to know that it is not merely an African American issue, but rather an issue that encompasses all types of cultural inequity, whether based on ethnicity, race, gender, age, geographic area, family, social class, time period, economics, or education. As long as any prejudice exists, civil rights will continue to pose moral and ethical dilemmas.

Space Exploration

Purpose

As a result of completing the activities on this Bloom sheet, the students will demonstrate growth in the following areas:

1. constructing a time line;

2. analyzing the effects of technology on the global community;

3. applying the knowledge of how and why people discover, utilize, and consume resources in the public interest; and

4. using a graphic organizer to summarize information.

Knowledge: [Search for information about why satellites stay in orbit. Present your findings on a poster or chart.] Answers will vary. A somewhat oversimplified explanation is this: when a satellite is propelled into space to a point at which its movement by centrifugal force (curvilinear movement away from the earth) is counterbalanced by the amount of gravitational pull, the satellite is in orbit. (Gravitational pull is the opposite of centrifugal force and is known as centripetal force).

PUMP PRIMER ─────────

For some students, this is a difficult concept, made more difficult by the technical language of science texts. A simple demonstration might be the best way to achieve understanding. Take students to a place where a ball can be safely thrown. Have a student volunteer throw the ball as levelly as possible. Note how far it goes before it hits the ground. Ask students why it hit the ground at all and did not just continue in a straight path (gravity). Then ask the students how to go about throwing the ball further. Probe until someone volunteers the idea of *loft* (the upward course, or arc, of an object driven into space). Ask why this works (distance lessens gravitational pull). Ask what would happen if you could toss the ball so far out that gravity no longer had significant pull but was not totally absent (orbit). Allow students to experiment with tossing the ball. Have them note at what point the loft actually works against the increase in distance. Have them speculate on whether the results would be different if the ball were hit by a bat rather than merely thrown (yes). Lead them to discover that another ingredient in the mix is *force*—supplied to the satellite by the rockets that propel it into space. Yet another is *speed*. Have students discover the speed necessary to overcome gravitational pull (25,000 mph).

Comprehension: [Prepare a time line having at least ten events that are significant in the history of space exploration.] Answers will vary. Among the items students might choose from for their ten events are these:

10/4/57: First artificial satellite launched. (*Sputnik*, USSR)

4/12/61: First man in space. (Yuri Gagarin, *Vostok 1*, USSR)

5/5/61: First American in space. (Alan Shepard, *Mercury 2*, US)

2/20/62: First American in orbit. (John Glenn, *Mercury 6*, US):

6/16/63: First woman in space. (Valentina Tereshkova, *Vostok 6*, USSR)

3/18/65: First space walk. (Alexei Leonov, *Voskhod 2*, USSR)

3/16/66: First space docking. (*Gemini 8* with unmanned Gemini Agena Target Vehicle; emergency splashdown, US)

1/27/67: First US loss of life. (*Apollo 1* command module ignites during launch practice, killing Gus Grissom, Ed White, and Roger Chaffee, US)

12/21/68: First manned flight around the moon. (Frank Borman, James Lovell, William Anders, *Apollo 8*, US)

7/20/69: First men on the moon. (Neil Armstrong and Edward "Buzz" Aldrin land in *Eagle* Lunar Module while Michael Collins stays aboard *Apollo 11*, US)

4/19/71: First orbital space station launched. (*Salyut 1*, destroyed 10/11/71, after approx. 2800 orbits, USSR);

4/12/81: First space shuttle mission. (*Columbia Space Transportation System*, US)

4/4/83: Communications satellite launched from space shuttle. (*Challenger 6*, US)

6/18/63: First US woman in space. (Sally Ride with four other astronauts aboard *Challenger 7*, US)

1/28/86: First US space disaster; first American of Asian

descent in space. (*Challenger* explosion just after lift-off kills astronauts Dick Scobee, Mike Smith, Ellison Omzuka, Ron McNair, Judy Reznik, and civilians Gregory Jarvis and Christa McAuliffe, US)

1992: First African-American woman astronaut. (Dr. Mae Jemison, aboard *Spacelab-J*)

8/18/93: First reusable rocket launched. (*Delta Clipper*, US)

There are, of course, numerous other significant dates, going back to the early work in rocketry done about the turn of the century by such pioneers as Konstantin Tsilkovsky, Dr. Robert Goddard, and Hermann Oberth, and continuing to the present. Accept whatever events students select if they can justify them as significant.

PUMP PRIMER

If you are using this sheet for whole-class instruction, it might be worthwhile to divide the class into two research groups (USSR and US) and allow them to discover these highlights and the facts regarding them. Students could then be given 9 × 12 sheets of tagboard and asked to make a cutout symbol representing each of the various missions. It could be a representation of the spacecraft, but should not be limited to that. These cutouts could then have the important facts written on them and be hung on a wall as a time line or, if the facts are written on both sides, hung from the ceiling as a time line mobile. An alternative for students of varying ability levels or varying interest levels would be to divide into research, design, and presentation teams. It is important that every child have a role

requiring individual accountability.

Application: [Trace the development of NASA from the end of World War II to its establishment by law on July 29, 1958.] Answers will vary. An important aspect of the development of the U.S. space program is that following World War II, each branch of the military was working separately and sometimes secretly on rocketry and space exploration projects. It was only after the launch of *Sputnik I* that the Congress set up a civilian-oriented agency to coordinate these efforts. Eisenhower sent the endorsement to Congress on April 2, 1958, and by July 29 the National Aeronautics and Space Act had become law.

Analysis: [Examine the roles of natural resources, economic prosperity, highly developed technology, and massive land areas in the space race. From your data draw conclusions about why other nations did not participate in the race to the moon.] Most answers should be accepted if reasoning is valid. However, it may be important to point out that it was a specific combination of factors that made the two superpowers contestants. Nations that had only some of the key ingredients did not participate. Canada, for example, had everything but the cold war; Iraq was wealthy enough but lacked technological sophistication and land; England lacked land and natural resources.

Analysis: [The first Soviet woman in space made her historic flight twenty years before NASA sent a woman into space.

Make a list of cultural differences that might account for this disparity.] You may wish to point out that the space program in America was very much a closed society of white males for decades, and, following the pattern set in other civil rights arenas, even minority males gained acceptance before women did. Part of this may be due to a male-as-protector cultural bias that continues to dominate in many areas of American life. Even in the *Challenger* disaster, there is inequity in that it is Christa McAuliffe, the civilian woman, who became the folk hero, despite the fact that six others died with her.

Synthesis: [Develop a projection of future events in America's space program.] Answers will vary. Procedures for sharing these projections might include oral or written reports, charts or posters, or multimedia reports. Projections should not significantly contradict current NASA plans.

PUMP PRIMER

Students may be interested in joining the Young Astronaut Council. Founded in 1984, the council is a private non-profit national educational program. Members may compete in contests and on projects designed to promote science, mathematics, and technology.

Evaluation: [The destruction by fire of Apollo 1 and the 1986 explosion of a *Challenger* STS cost the lives of ten U.S. space explorers, including two who were not traditionally trained astronauts. Decide whether the advancements afforded by the space program are sufficient to justify this loss of human life. Defend your position in an editorial.] Answers will vary. Before making their decisions, students might need to investigate, singly or in groups, technological advancements that came about because of space exploration problem-solving.

CONNECTING TO MYTHOLOGY

Not only do many of the planets carry names from Greco-Roman mythology, but the early U.S. space projects had mythological names: Mercury, Gemini, Apollo. Have students discover who these figures were and speculate on (or research) why these names were used for these missions.

CONNECTING TO SCIENCE

The connections to science are numerous, ranging from something as simple as studying sonic booms (created by space-craft reentering the earth's atmosphere) to something as complex as building model rockets.

CONNECTING TO HEALTH/ FITNESS

Students might be interested in discovering the rigorous fitness standards required of astronauts. (Have them speculate on why Al Shepard was grounded by inner ear problems, separating his flights by ten years.)

They might also like to investigate the early practice of quarantining returning astronauts. (Astronauts were pulled from their splash-down locations and were washed down with disinfectant to kill "lunar bugs" before being allowed even to board the rescue helicopter. On board ship, they were taken to a mobile quarantine facility connected to the world at large by a minimal support staff and by the view afforded them through a picture window. Once back in Houston, they finished out their three-week decontamination inside a biological barrier known as a Lunar Receiving Laboratory.)

There is also some question as to how space travel itself affects health. Returning astronauts generally experience bloated heads, engorged neck veins, blood thinning, nausea, dizziness, fainting spells, and other side effects. And though astronauts are in top physical health when they start their missions, some—but not all—are plagued by health problems after their return. The most notable case is that of Jim Irwin. After one of his excursions, biomedical feedback data indicated some cardiac arrhythmia. Doctors decided at the time that Irwin's space diet was to blame, and subsequent flights included massive infusions of potassium in an effort to prevent chemical imbalances. Irwin, however, was to experience continuing problems with heart irregularities and heart attacks.

CONNECTING TO LITERATURE

NASA invited Anne Morrow Lindbergh to record her impressions of the Apollo 11 mission. Have students read all or part of her account. Theorize why NASA might want to have a writer's viewpoint added to the scientific viewpoint. During this same mission, the astronauts chose to broadcast as part of their Christmas Day message an excerpt from the book of Genesis. Have students speculate about their choice–why the Bible? Why a quote from Genesis instead of the Christmas story? Did this violate the principle of separation of church and state?

CONNECTING TO MATHEMATICS

Have students use their calculators to figure the travel time needed to get to the various planets, using the formula $T = D/R$, where T = time, D = distance from earth to the planet, and R = 25,000 miles per hour, the speed needed to break free of the earth's gravity. Have them recalculate with R = 150,000 mph, the maximum speed of existing spacecraft. They can also translate the distances from miles to astronomical units, where one AU = 93 million miles (the approximate mean distance of the sun from the earth). Remind them that they can simplify the task by striking six zeroes and dividing by 93.

EXTENDING THE STUDY

Students might enjoy reading June Behrens's *Sally Ride, Astronaut.*

Airplanes and Automobiles

Purpose

As a result of completing the activities on this Bloom sheet, the students will demonstrate growth in the following areas:

1. analyzing the relationship of people, places, and events in the past and their effects on both the present and the future;

2. interpreting how changes in transportation influence the rates at which people, goods, and ideas move from place to place;

3. identifying the importance of technology as a catalyst for change; and

4. explaining the impact of an individual on historical development.

Knowledge: [Place each of the following names under the heading Airplanes or Automobiles: Henry Ford, Charles A. Lindbergh, Charles E. and J. Frank Duryea, Glenn H. Curtiss, Jacqueline Cochran, and Frances E. and Freelan O. Stanley.]

Airplanes: Charles A. Lindbergh, Glenn H. Curtiss, and Jacqueline Cochran. Automobiles: Henry Ford, Charles E. and J. Frank Duryea, and Francis E. and Freelan O. Stanley.

Comprehension: [Explain the contribution each person above made to either the automobile or the airline industry.]

Charles A. Lindbergh flew nonstop from New York to Paris.

Glenn H. Curtiss built the first successful seaplane.

Jacqueline Cochran set the world speed record for women in 1937.

Henry Ford introduced the assembly line in the manufacture of automobiles.

Charles E. and J. Frank Duryea built a roofless motor buggy in 1893.

Francis E. and Freelan O. Stanley built the first steam-driven car.

Comprehension: [Explain the term barnstormer.] Barnstormers were daredevil pilots who flew stunts at county fairs and performed aerial acrobatic acts. Due to the lack of air fields, pilots often landed in cow pastures or fields of stubble—hence the name. After a performance, barnstormers often sold rides to people who longed to experience flight.

Application: [Choose one of the following activities.

a) Sketch an automobile or an airplane.

b) Construct a model car or plane and bring it in to show the class.

c) Produce a pamphlet to show the development of either the automobile or the airplane.

d) Estimate the cost of owning an automobile today. Collect necessary information including purchase price and cost of insurance, license plates, gasoline, and maintenance, and present the information in outline form.] Work will vary.

Analysis: [Determine the changes in American life caused by the automobile and airplane.] Americans longed for increased mobility. The automobile offered this mobility, and with it the opportunity for jobs and a chance to visit relatives—even out of state. People left the farms and headed to the cities. Air travel also increased Americans' mobility because faster travel

was possible. Air mail service increased communication both at home and abroad.

There was also a negative impact on society. Highway deaths increased and commerce in the cities suffered due to the construction of shopping centers and malls in the suburbs.

Synthesis: [Make up a new ad campaign for your favorite auto.] Work will vary.

Evaluation: [Devise three improvements in automobile and/or airplane safety.] Answers will vary.

American Cities

Purpose

As a result of completing the activities on this Bloom sheet, the students will demonstrate growth in the following areas:

1. utilizing globes and a variety of maps as primary geographic research tools;

2. locating places using absolute location;

3. identifying the importance of technology as a catalyst for change;

4. applying a decision-making process; and

5. identifying the appropriate sources to obtain information using print materials and technology.

Knowledge: [Name five large U.S. cities.] Answers and work will vary.

It may be best to assign a specific area or state to students. This will prevent cities like Chicago, Los Angeles, and New York from being selected by everyone.

Comprehension: [Compare your cities in size and population. Reorganize your list of cities based on population. Determine the location of these cities on a map, and cite their latitudes and longitudes.] Answers and work will vary.

Application: [Investigate the growth of cities between 1870 and 1900. Collect information and be prepared to discuss your findings with the class.] Answers and work will vary.

Students should know that by 1910, at least half of all Americans lived in cities. Cities attracted newcomers because of all they had to offer, including lights, various modes of transportation, indoor plumbing, and even a wider variety of fruits and vegetables.

Encourage students to read about the changes that took place between 1870 and 1900. Many foreigners who settled in cities searched for employment and a better way of life.

Analysis: [Identify problems connected to city life. Survey a group of ten classmates to discover which problem is viewed as the most serious.] Answers and work will vary.

Encourage students to research problems that existed in the past as well as problems existing in today's cities. For example, between 1870 and 1880, the cities were quite literally stinky,

due to the horse manure on the streets (hundreds of tons a day)! Pollution of water and air existed early in our society. Crime, street gangs, suicide, and alcoholism were problems then as they are now.

Synthesis: [Create a collage of pictures and words that reflect the sights and sounds of city life.] Answers and work will vary.

Have students contact travel agencies and auto clubs for brochures about U.S. cities. If time is not crucial, they could also write the chamber of commerce in several cities.

Evaluation: [Contrast life in the city to life in the country. Decide where you would prefer to live. Support your decision with a minimum of three reasons.] Answers and work will vary.

PUMP PRIMER

Take advantage of the quick, simplified approach offered by using children's books. Read aloud two books, one depicting city life (e.g., *Come in the Morning* by Mary Harris) and one depicting rural life (e.g., *Reuben and the Fire* by Pat Buckley Moss and Merle Good). Compare the two lifestyles as presented in the stories. This could be done prior to the evaluation activity, to give students insights into whichever lifestyle is least familiar to them before they have to make the decision called for by the activity.

CONNECTING TO ART

Students may wish to learn more about the skyscrapers of the 1880s and about Louis H. Sullivan, who helped rebuild the

city of Chicago after the Great Fire of 1871.

Attractions

Purpose

As a result of completing the activities on this Bloom sheet, the students will demonstrate growth in the following areas:

1. organizing information in brochure and poster formats;

2. identifying the appropriate source for obtaining information using print materials and technology; and

3. identifying likenesses and differences in dissimilar data.

Knowledge: [Choose five brochures for places to visit. List the names and locations of the attractions described in them.] Brochures advertising attractions are usually easy to obtain simply by visiting a travel agency, AAA, an attraction, a hotel, larger restaurants, a tourist welcome center, or a chamber of commerce. Most such places will have racks with brochures from all over the state or the surrounding area and you can get what you need all in one place. If you prefer, have your students scout around for brochures or have them write to the state travel and tourism department and ask for brochures.

Comprehension: [Read a brochure of your choice. Reword the information given. Use your write-up as you design a poster to

advertise the attraction.]
Responses will vary.

Application: [Find more information about one of the cities listed. Locate the city on a map and record a minimum of five facts about the city or its attractions.] Answers will vary

Analysis: [Compare three brochures. What do they have in common? What are their differences?] Commonalities will probably include such things as best-foot-forward imaging, positive wording, maps, hours of operation, costs, and so on.

Synthesis: [Arrange the information given to create a whole new look to the advertisement. Design a new cover.] Products will vary.

Evaluation: [Using your brochures, choose a vacation destination for your family. Justify your decision.] Answers will vary.

PUMP PRIMER

This is a good place to work in a strong connection to life skills in mathematics. After students choose a vacation destination, have them work up a budget—or several budgets. They might enter such variables as mode of transportation (car, train, boat, plane), length of stay, lodging (luxury hotel, quality motel, budget motel, rented cabin, efficiency, RV, camping), and food costs. They might also develop a "bare bones" version and an optimal version.

Canals, Rivers, and Roads

Purpose

As a result of completing the activities on this Bloom sheet, the student will demonstrate growth in the following areas:

1. obtaining appropriate information from indexes, tables of contents, dictionary entries, and the like;

2. utilizing appropriate decision-making skills to design a town;

3. explaining how and why people move themselves, their products, and their ideas across the earth; and

4. interpreting how changes in transportation influenced the rates at which people, goods, and ideas moved from place to place.

Knowledge: [Label the following on a map of the United States: National Road, Lancaster Turnpike, the Erie Canal, the Pennsylvania Main Line Canal, the Missouri River, the Ohio River, and the Mississippi River.] Students should be able to correct of their work using available textbooks, atlases, or encyclopedias.

Comprehension: [List the merits and drawbacks of rivers, roads, and canals for transporting agricultural products and manufactured goods.] Roads made travel easier between established towns, but roadways wore out and repairs were costly. Rivers were an acceptable means

of north-south travel, but merchants wanted an east-west route because it would help keep shipping costs down. Canals were a means of water transportation that proved to be too slow. With the coming of the railroads, which could go anywhere, the canals largely became obsolete.

Application: [Develop a news story announcing the completion of the Erie Canal. Be as specific with facts as possible.] The stories should include the following: In 1816 DeWitt Clinton, governor of New York, initiated the Erie Canal Project. Work began in 1817 and was completed in 1825. The Erie Canal was forty feet wide and four feet deep and had eighty-four locks. It connected the Great Lakes to the Atlantic Ocean.

Analysis: [Determine the changes caused by steamboats to the system of transporting goods.] Steam transport reduced shipping costs, increased the speed of delivery and travel, and allowed for two-way commerce on United States rivers.

Synthesis: [Create your own town. Draw a map showing major roads, waterways, and places of interest. Your town may be from the past, the present, or the future. Be sure to label items and/or make a key. Write a descriptive report to accompany your drawing.] Work will vary.

Evaluation: [You are a western farmer in the 1800s. Choose a method for transporting your goods to a market in the East. Give reasons for your choice.] Answers will vary.

CONNECTING TO MUSIC

Students may enjoy investigating the numerous songs that have been written about various forms of transportation and about individual rivers, roads, and canals. Have them speculate about our romantic attachments to these passageways and decide what they symbolize to most people.

EXTENDING THE STUDY

Have students look at the highways and waterways in their area. See if they can discover the connections between these corridors and the development of towns and commercial centers. In the case of man-made corridors such as roads and canals, students may be able to discover what natural features influenced the choice of route, what political issues were raised by their construction, and what impact they had (and continue to have) on local economy.

Careers

Purpose

As a result of completing the activities on this Bloom sheet, the students will demonstrate growth in the following areas:

1. investigating careers;

2. interviewing techniques;

3. consolidating information taken from a variety of sources into a new product; and

4. identifying the appropriate sources to obtain information using print materials and technology.

Knowledge: [List the fifteen career areas that encompass most careers.] According to the U.S. Office of Education, the fifteen career clusters are

- Agri-business/Natural Resources
- Business and Office
- Communication and Media
- Construction
- Consumer/Homemaking Education
- Environment
- Fine Arts and Humanities
- Health
- Hospitality and Recreation
- Manufacturing
- Marine Science
- Marketing and Distribution
- Personal Services
- Public Service
- Transportation

Comprehension: [Generate a list of careers being considered by members of your group. If necessary, poll other groups until your list totals twenty-five or more possible careers. Place each of these careers in the appropriate fifteen career area.] Suggested answers:

AGRI-BUSINESS/NATURAL RESOURCES

rancher
florist
mining engineer
farmer
breeder

landscaper

BUSINESS AND OFFICE

key punch operator
accountant
court reporter
secretary
small business owner

COMMUNICATION AND MEDIA

reporter
librarian
editor
radio air personality

CONSTRUCTION

roofer
carpenter
architect
plumber
brick layer
plasterer
crane operator
steeplejack
electrician
glass cutter
air conditioning specialist
metal worker

CONSUMER/HOMEMAKING EDUCATION

dietitian
industrial home economist
food-store owner
fashion designer

ENVIRONMENT

forester
city planner
ranger
sanitary engineer
pollution control expert

FINE ARTS AND HUMANITIES

commercial artist
illustrator
anthropologist
novelist
cartoonist
musician

HEALTH

pharmacist
veterinarian
optometrist
dental hygienist

HOSPITALITY AND RECREATION

travel agent
restaurant owner
ski instructor
chef

MANUFACTURING

welder
production manager
inspector
assembly line worker

MARINE SCIENCE

marine biologist
oceanographer
science teacher
commercial fishery

MARKETING AND DISTRIBUTION

buyer
ad copy writer
store manager
market research

PERSONAL SERVICES

barber
TV repair technician
lawyer
interior decorator

PUBLIC SERVICE

teacher
youth worker
politician
weather forecaster

TRANSPORTATION

traffic engineer
truck driver
flight attendant
automotive executive

Application: [Produce a pamphlet that shows the career opportunities available in any one field.] Products will vary.

PUMP PRIMER ————

Encourage students to do an I-search. This involves interviewing someone who works in the chosen career field and asking the person to check for accuracy in the pamphlet and also to suggest more ideas.

PUMP PRIMER ————

Consider arranging a display of the pamphlets in the school media center or placing the pamphlets in the guidance office. If your school or classroom has a community/business partnership in place, perhaps your partner would underwrite professional publication of one or more pamphlets or would assist in wider distribution.

Analysis: [Investigate one career of your choosing to discover the education, skills, and attributes that are desirable for a person pursuing that career.] Decide on a presentation format that fits the time and space available. Again, an interview with a person working in the field would be a helpful source.

Synthesis: [Speculate about what would happen if suddenly there were no workers in your chosen career field.] Answers will vary. Students should be made aware that this may not be an improbability: futurists predict that most students will have to retrain for new careers up to seven times during their lifetime, and often it will be because technology has eliminated their old jobs.

Evaluation: [Examine the fifteen career areas and decide which will be important in the next century. Rank the areas in order from most important to least important. Justify your choices.] Accept any order so long as answers are justified.

ADDITIONAL TEACHER RESOURCES

"Exploring Careers: 15 Full-Color Study Posters," Middle Upper Levels WC#951–053 ICM#571 Jackson, TN: Weber Costello (Instructor Curriculum Materials), n.d.

Computers

Purpose

As a result of completing the activities on this Bloom sheet, the students will demonstrate growth in the following areas:

1. exploring the impact of computers on career choices;

2. analyzing the effects of technology on the global community; and

3. organizing information in a visual format.

Knowledge: [Diagram and label the computer on which you are working.] Answers will vary. At a minimum, students should be able to identify the keyboard, the disk drive(s), the hard drive, the monitor, and the printer. Peripherals such as modems and number pads should be included if they are part of the student's experience.

Comprehension: [Explain the following terms relative to computers:]

Qwerty keyboard: The standard keyboard used by most typewriter and computer manufacturers. The arrangement is designed to accommodate the most frequent patterns of letter usage by placing them within easy reach of the index fingers and relegating less frequently used letters to positions covered by the weaker fingers. The name comes from the left side of the top line of letters and is pronounced as a two-syllable word. Students should be aware that some hand-held computers/organizers still have an alphabetic keyboard.

WYSIWYG: An acronym (pronounced "whizz-ee-wig") for "what you see is what you get," meaning that the screen display exactly reflects the printed document.

Gigo: Pronounced as separate letters, gigo stands for "garbage in/garbage out." Gigo indicates that the computer is incapable of producing results better than

the data entered into the computer.

Upload/download: The process of launching (starting) or quitting a program.

On-line: Connected to a system or network of computers.

Justify: To adjust the spaces between words to align margins evenly. Many computer programs do this automatically.

Options: Choices presented by the program being used.

Program: An application written in language the computer can understand providing specific instructions that produce specific effects.

Disk: A circular piece of plastic coated with iron oxide on which applications are prerecorded or to which you may record your own data.

Application: [Write a script for explaining to a computer novice how to load, run, and shut down a program of your choice.] Work will vary.

It might be beneficial to pair experienced students up with novice users and have the tutors compose their scripts as they go through an application. That way, language that is too technical or directions that are unclear can be detected and remedied immediately. If all the students in your school are computer literate to some degree, have students invite parents, grandparents, or neighbors in for a "free computer lesson." Or, you could invite the nearest senior center or retirement home to send volunteers to work with the children.

Analysis: [On a diagram or poster, depict how the computer is like a typewriter, a tape recorder, a television, a photocopier, a file cabinet, and a musical synthesizer.] Products will vary. To extend this activity, have students point out differences between the computer and each of these other items. You could also have them think of other items whose function has been incorporated into computers, such as calculators, address books, memo pads, calendars, and sketch books.

Synthesis: [Choose a career field that interests you and determine how computers are used in that field. Prepare a poster or brochure explaining the importance of computer literacy with regard to this career.] Results will vary. You may want to suggest that students conduct telephone interviews with people who work in their chosen field, that they visit workplaces of those in their chosen careers, and/or that they talk to schools or colleges about computer use in this field. They might also consult secondary sources such as magazine articles or reference books.

Evaluation: [Draw up a set of rules or laws that you think should govern computer use worldwide. Rank in order the top five and tell why you believe them to be crucial.] Answers will vary. As a prewriting exercise, you might want to have students discuss such issues as international copyrights, rights of privacy, national security issues, and the like.

The Environment

Purpose

As a result of completing the activities on this Bloom sheet, the students will demonstrate growth in the following areas:

1. awareness of environmental issues;

2. sensitivity to current concerns affecting the environment;

3. identifying the appropriate sources to obtain information using print materials and technology;

4. explaining the impact of an individual on historical development; and

5. identifying the positive and negative effects of human alteration of physical environments.

Knowledge: [Collect newspaper articles, magazine articles, and pictures that deal with environmental issues.] Work will vary. You may wish to specify a minimum number of items.

Knowledge: [Define the following: endangered species, the greenhouse effect, pollution, recycle, ozone layer, fluorocarbon, landfill, smog, biodegradable, and rain forest.] Definitions are readily available from a variety of sources, including most dictionaries.

Comprehension: [Explain how President Theodore Roosevelt acted as a conservationist while in office.] Roosevelt was personally interested in the conserva-tion of our natural resources. He added more than 140 million acres to the national forests. In 1905, he created the National Forest Service and appointed Gifford Pinchot as its director.

Comprehension: [Choose one of the vocabulary words from the second "Knowledge" activity and illustrate the definition in the form of a cartoon.] Work will vary.

Application: [Make a collage using the items collected for the first "Knowledge" task.] Work will vary.

Analysis: [Write an informative speech on local or state environmental concerns and the programs initiated to address them.] Work will vary.

Synthesis: [Design a poster that encourages people to recycle.] Work will vary.

Evaluation: [Persuade others that the environment needs to be cared for. Write a letter to the editor of your local paper. Be sure to include your purpose in writing and facts learned from your research and from class discussions.] Letters should be collected and previewed by the teacher. Select several to send to the local paper. Due to space constraints and editorial policies, your paper may not be able to print everyone's views. Consider including a few letters in the next parent newsletter or arranging to display the letters in your local library.

Connecting to Literature

There are numerous literary works dealing with the environ-ment that appeal to transescent students. Among them are these:

Joy Adamson, *Born Free*

Paul Annixter, "Last Cover"

Natalie Babbitt, *Tuck Everlast-ing*

Pearl S. Buck, "The Old Demon"

Chief Seattle, "Letter to the U.S. Government"

John Ciardi, "The Shark"

Elizabeth Coatsworth, "Wilderness Rivers"

Robert P. Tristram Coffin, "The Pheasant"

Jack Cope, "Power"

Emily Dickinson, "How Soft a Caterpillar Steps"

E-Yeh-Shure, "Beauty"

Margery Facklam, "Belle Benchley: Zoo Director"

_____ "Eugenie Clark & the Sleeping Sharks"

Paul Fleischman, "Fireflies"

Robert Frost, "Dust of Snow"

_____ "The Pasture"

_____ "Stopping by Woods on a Snowy Evening"

Jean Craighead George, "The Hatchling Turtles"

Nikki Giovanni, "Winter Poem"

Langston Hughes, "April Rain Song"

Juan Ramon Jimenez, "Light and Water/Luz y Aqua"

Myra Cohn Livingston, "Sea Songs"

Jack London, "The King of Mazy May"

Phyllis McGinley, "Season at the Shore"

Eve Merriam, "Simile: Willow and Ginkgo"

Sheryl L. Nelms, "Cumulus Clouds"

Richard Peck, "The Geese"

Jack Prelutsky, "Ankylosaurus"

Horacio Quiroga, "How the Flamingoes Got Their Stockings"

Marjorie Kinnan Rawlings, "Rattlesnake Hunt"

Wilson Rawls, *Where the Red Fern Grows*

James W. Riley, "When the Frost Is on the Punkin"

Theodore Roethke, "The Bat"

William Saroyan, "The Hummingbird That Lived Through the Winter"

Leslie Marmon Silko, "Humaeepi, the Warrior Priest"

Shel Silverstein, "Sarah Cynthia Sylvia Stout"

William Jay Smith, "Seal"

James Stephens, "Washed in Silver"

Jesse Stuart, "Old Ben"

May Swenson, "Cat and the Weather"

Edwin Way Teale, "Circle of the Seasons"

James Ramsey Ullman, "A Boy and a Man"

Walt Whitman, "Miracles"

Valerie Worth, "Sun"

Laurence Yep, "Breaker's Bridge"

Field Trip

Purpose

As a result of completing the activities on this Bloom sheet, the students will demonstrate growth in the following areas:

1. distinguishing fact from opinion; and

2. identifying the appropriate source to obtain information using print materials and technology.

Knowledge: [Recall ten facts about the field trip. You may include specific facts about the trip as well as descriptions of time spent with friends.] Answers and work will vary.

Comprehension: [List five ways in which the trip related to class lessons and discussions.] Answers and work will vary.

Application: [Organize a field trip for your class. Determine the destination, means of travel, cost, and times of departure, arrival, and return to school. Record all information and be prepared to share with the class.] Answers and work will vary.

The work task may be compiled in a grade level, team, or school resource handbook.

Analysis: [Select three locations in your area that would be desirable for a class field trip. Survey classmates to determine their preferences. Graph your results.] Answers and work will vary.

Involve students in setting up educational objectives for the field trips they propose. Students (and sometimes their parents) need to be aware that field trips are not just a day out of school, but that they address learning concerns in a unique way.

Consider having students research what other towns, cities, and states have to offer. An interdisciplinary approach involving all academic areas, art, and vocational classes would be effective.

Synthesis: [Imagine you are on the tourist board and have the responsibility of increasing the number of visitors to your area. Design a pamphlet or poster that profiles areas of interest in your city or state.] Answers and work will vary.

Evaluation: [Interpret the graph results (from the analysis task) of another student. Write a brief summary of the results.] Answers and work will vary.

Evaluation: [Recommend an area of interest that you would like to explore on a future field trip. Support the recommendation with three to five reasons.] Answers and work will vary.

Students could be given an imaginary starting budget for planning their field trips. Not enough money for a trip to Washington, D.C. (or Washington state)? Allow students to be problem solvers. Do they try to earn more money for this particular trip or select a destination that is within their means?

Students could plan a year-long field trip to study American history. Where would the trip begin? Routes could be selected and information gathered on the various destinations. Imagine the fun and excitement created by this imaginary trip.

From Melting Pot to Salad Bowl: Multicultural America

Purpose

As a result of completing the activities on this Bloom sheet, the students will demonstrate growth in the following areas:

1. explaining why various cultural groups immigrated in the past;

2. articulating the influence on and contributions of cultural groups to America's national heritage;

3. explaining how a location's significance changes as cultures alter their interactions with each other and the physical environment;

4. working independently and cooperatively within groups to accomplish goals; and

5. demonstrating a knowledge of place and location by creating a map.

Knowledge: [On a map of the United States, locate ten or more ethnic communities. Compare your map with at least three others, making whatever additions or corrections are needed.] You may want to require no more than one locale per state in students' initial efforts, to guarantee that students extend their study beyond the limits of their own state or city. You might suggest such ethnic communities

as Indian reservations, Chinatown in San Francisco, Eskimo communities in Alaska, the Greek community at Tarpon Springs, Florida, the Amish and Mennonite communities in Pennsylvania, Japanese communities in Hawaii, the Hispanic barrios of San Antonio, Los Angeles, and New York, the Russian influx in Glen Ullin, North Dakota, or the settlement of Dutch railroad workers at Zwolle, Louisiana.

Comprehension: [Choose a culture other than your own and report on where the people of that culture settled, why they chose that spot, how they contributed to the unique character of the area, and at least one craft or food they brought with them and popularized.] Answers will vary. Although you will probably want to emphasize positive assimilations, you may need to discuss students' negative perceptions of other assimilations, such as their feelings about illegal immigrants from Vietnam, Mexico, Cuba, or Haiti. Have them identify what it is that they fear or distrust about these groups before asking them to identify how these groups differ from other, more positive, examples, and even from other groups of the same ethnic origin who emigrated legally and at a different time. Point out that it is often easier to have historical empathy than present-minded acceptance of groups: once a group of immigrants have established themselves as hard-working contributors to American society, we accept them more easily. Open discussion might lead to why one group of immigrants is

more readily accepted than another.

Application: [Make a book or video about multiculturalism in your own community, county, or state.] Suggest that students include information on lifestyles, family values, costumes or styles of dress, customs, art, music, and language for each culture represented. Where possible, students might add photos, drawings, or magazine cutouts to their books as illustrations.

Analysis: [A culture can be defined as any group that is joined by common goals, needs, and/or belief systems. As such, each of us is multicultural, belonging to many cultures at once. Brainstorm a list of elements of typical cultures.] Answers will vary. Brainstorming could be done with the class as a whole, using a word web or think-pair-share.

A word web puts the target word (*culture*) at the center of a wheel and uses free association to add words at the ends of spokes around the wheel. The process is repeated with each of the spoke words, until a well-defined list is concocted. The resultant list bears a strong resemblance to a spider's web, with lines connecting words in every direction.

Think-pair-share is a cooperative brainstorming technique that encourages students to work first alone, then in pairs, and then in groups of four or six, the objective being to expand each person's list at each step. Segments are timed and students are encouraged to work rapidly. A whole-class sharing session can follow the last segment. Word webs and think-pair-share are described in more detail in the answer key to the Writers Who Shaped History sheet.

Synthesis: [Devise a game that requires players to make choices about tolerance and understanding. Remember to add an element of luck to keep the game challenging.] Students might experience more success if allowed to work in pairs or triads. Depending on the ability levels of students, you might want to suggest that they take an existing game board and change the rules. For example, a simple game like "Chutes and Ladders" or "Parchesi" could be modified with choice cards supplementing the spinner or replacing the dice. Each card might contain a moral dilemma in multiple-choice format. Depending on the option chosen, a student might be allowed to move a specific number of spaces forward or to double or triple a roll on the "Parchesi" board or to ascend a ladder or not slide down a chute in "Chutes and Ladders." Remind students, too, that games do not have to be board games. Some students might prefer to devise games that involve physical activity and/or athletic skill.

Evaluation: [Decide which five elements of culture are most important and rank them. Give reasons for your choices.] Answers will vary.

Evaluation: [Make a list of ways America is (or was) like a melting pot and another list of ways she is (or was) like a salad bowl. Which do you think is the more nearly accurate image today? Why?] The melting pot analogy has a historical context that should be readily understood by most students. The salad bowl analogy is newer and, thus, seldom explained in textbooks: in a salad bowl, although the mixture is complete and pleasing, each item retains its separate identity and unique characteristics—something that doesn't happen in a melting pot.

Handicaps

Purpose

As a result of completing the activities on this Bloom sheet, students will demonstrate growth in the following areas:

1. describing some of the challenges and benefits of living handicapped in today's society;

2. showing how handicaps can both connect people and cause misunderstandings;

3. applying a decision-making process to the understanding of an unfamiliar lifestyle; and

4. explaining how various people experience the world in different ways or from different points of view.

Knowledge: [List the provisions of Public Law 94–142 and the Americans with Disabilities Act.]

Public Law 94–142 is an amendment to the Education for Handicapped Children Act. It provides that handicapped students have the right to a free and appropriate education in the least restrictive environment (LRE). Provisions include the following:

- Services to meet special needs must be provided by the school system.

- Students should be taught among non-handicapped students whenever possible.

- Parents must have prior knowledge of all evaluation procedures.

- Parents may refuse evaluation and/or services.

- Test results must be explained to parents.

- Parents may obtain independent evaluations and these may, under special circumstances, be conducted at school expense.

- Parents have access to and limited control over all records kept by the school.

- School records must be private, and parents are entitle to know who has access to them.

- Parents are entitled to due process hearings when they disagree with the school's decisions regarding placement or services.

- Communication with parents must be conducted in a language (including sign language) understandable to the parent.

The Americans with Disabilities Act of 1990 (ADA) mandates the elimination of discrimination against individuals with disabilities. Although there are four sections, only two seem to affect schools: the section on programs, services, and facilities and the section on hiring practices.

The act's major provisions state that the disabled

- cannot be denied programs, activities, or services because of their disability;

- cannot be provided with separate but unequal programs;

- must at their request be allowed access to regular programs, even when separate programs are in place;

- must have reasonable access to existing facilities and must be accommodated in the design of new facilities;

- must be adequately provided for with respect to communication, including the use of TDD's (telecommunications devices for the deaf); and

- cannot be discriminated against in employment.

Comprehension: [Brainstorm a list of at least fifteen visible and invisible handicaps that affect schoolchildren.] Lists will vary. You may want to compile a master list and post it. It would probably be a good idea to devote some time to discussing the more obscure handicaps.

Pump Primer ————————

You may want to allow a lot of latitude in deciding what handicaps "affect schoolchildren." For example, although teen alcoholism is a burgeoning problem, teens can be equally handicapped by having an alcoholic parent. You may also want

to discuss what makes a handicap visible or invisible: the whole concept of an invisible handicap may be new to most students. (Heart disease is an example of an invisible handicap. One might never know another was handicapped by heart disease, but it has such effects as limiting physical activity and increasing school absenteeism.)

Application: [Choose a handicap to study in depth. Make a data tent to display your findings.] Products will vary. You may want to suggest that students use the front of the tent card for a picture or illustration and the back for data, or that they use the outside for pictures or illustrations and the inside for data. Urge students to seek out specific data, though they may not all be successful in all areas. Suggested areas include description of the disability, the types of people most susceptible, symptoms, treatment, visible manifestations, available statistics, and addresses of agencies or support groups.

Pump Primer ————————

There are various ways to construct a data tent, but the easiest is to use a file folder (one for each child), as file folders are sturdier than paper, and, unlike tagboard or poster paper, are already scored and folded. If you are using third- or fifth-cut folders, you'll need to trim the open edge. Folders should be at least 8" from fold to edge. Folders should be opened tent-style for display.

Analysis: [Keep a journal of the things you do for one week. Assess how being handicapped

would have affected those activities. Rewrite your journal as though you were physically or mentally challenged and wanted to have exactly the same week.] Answers will vary. Depending on the age and maturity of your students, you may want to adjust the number of days for which students are to record activities. In some instances, it may be more practical to have them list the things they do daily and then reconstruct from memory a list of the unusual activities they participated in during the last week.

Pump Primer ————————

This activity could prove too intense for some students under some circumstances. Consider sending home an informative letter before beginning this Bloom sheet, advising parents of the nature of the project and its rationale. Invite them to suggest areas their child might investigate or to let you know if there are areas they do not wish to have investigated. For example, if there's a history of cancer in a family, some children might find the investigation of cancer helps them cope, while others might find it devastating. Parent responses to the project can help alert you to problem areas in advance.

You will also want to be sensitive to the maladies and handicaps present within your class or school. Investigating cystic fibrosis might be interesting for some students, but if you have a student who suffers with CF, that child may be uncomfortable with *any* student's focusing on that disease as part of this project. A discreet inquiry can prevent problems early on. If a student does pursue an investigation of a condition affecting a classmate, close monitoring will be prudent.

Synthesis: [Produce a brochure about your handicap. Make it suitable for placement in the school's guidance office. Be sure to include addresses of national organizations that provide information and of any local support groups you discover.] Products will vary.

Evaluation: [Rank the handicaps studied by your class, listing them according to which you would find easiest to assume if you were forced to live forever with a handicap. Explain the rationale for at least your first and last choices.] Answers will vary.

CONNECTING TO LITERATURE

Students might gain empathy for the emotional battering some handicapped children experience by reading Felice Holman's *Slake's Limbo*.

Homelessness

Purpose

As a result of completing the activities on this Bloom sheet, the students will demonstrate growth in the following areas:

1. relating economic conditions to historical change;

2. evaluating the role of institutions in furthering both continuity and change; and

3. explaining the impact of an individual on historical development.

Knowledge: [Investigate the estimated number of homeless people in your area and state. Report to the class.] To simplify this task and to keep local agencies from being inundated by telephone calls and requests for information, you may want to divide students into research teams and give each the responsibility for checking with specific sources. Because resources differ from area to area, you will need to use the phone book and a good imagination to decide on your list of resources, but do not overlook such sources as the last census figures, the local newspaper, and the local school board. Once the list is made, students could draw the names from a bowl. Decide in advance whether you want agencies contacted by telephone or by mail. Have students devise a list of questions before contacting the agencies, and encourage them to follow up on any leads that are given them by the agencies.

PUMP PRIMER

Consider having one or more guest speakers bring the information to your classes and simply have students take notes. Again, a predetermined list of questions is essential.

Knowledge: [Summarize the 1987 Stewart B. McKinney Homeless Assistance Act.] This act is supposed to ensure access to a free public education for all homeless children. You may wish to have students inquire about your area's and state's efforts to comply with this act.

Comprehension: [Chart the effects of homelessness on your area and state.] Again, group efforts may be more efficient and less frustrating than individual effort. Considerations include welfare and AFDC costs, health care costs, lost revenue from real estate taxes and from tourism, education costs, lost tax dollars because of undercounting in censuses, and the drain on public charities.

Application: [IIllustrate a typical scene involving the homeless.] Products will vary. Although the information gathered in the previous activities should have given students new concepts for visualization, you may want to discuss in an open forum any stereotypes that seem prevalent. Students should understand that the homeless include more than "winos" and "bag ladies"; that sometimes entire families are homeless, that often the homeless are elderly, and that many migrant families are homeless in the strictest definition of the word. Teenagers who have run away from home seeking to outrun family problems often wind up homeless. Other factors that may affect who becomes homeless are the sudden loss of a job and an inability to acquire another, catastrophic illness, divorce, the imprisonment of the primary caretaker, and the like. Mature students may be ready to deal emotionally with the theory that many Americans are only two or three paychecks away from being homeless.

Analysis: [Research Jane Addams's opening of Hull House in Chicago in 1889. How did the problems Addams addressed compare with those that exist today?] Answers will vary.

Synthesis: [Propose a bill that would eliminate most of the educational barriers for homeless children.] Answers will vary. Students need to consider which of the existing barriers are remediable. While it may be possible to do away with proof of residency requirements, for example, or to provide free textbooks, immunizations, and clothing for needy students, it may be impossible to change the fact that a family concerned with food, shelter, and employment on a daily basis is rarely likely to make education a priority. Not every wrong can be redressed. Students also need to look at such things as cultural deprivation and to understand that a small child who has never been read to, has never sung children's songs or heard nursery rhymes, has never been exposed to childhood games is at an educational disadvantage from the start. Legislating against cultural deprivation is not likely to change anything, but legislating programs for culturally deprived children will affect everyone, either positively or negatively. (If students have difficulty seeing negative effects, have them look at the money trail and speculate on where that money might be spent if it were not being spent on Head Start or other pre-kindergarten programs.)

Evaluation: [List five or more factors that you believe are the key elements of homelessness and rank them in order of importance. Give reasons for your choices.] Answers will vary.

PUMP PRIMER ————

In less capable groupings of students, you may wish to brainstorm a list of factors, including such things as educational level of parents, number in family, employment opportunities, transportation (or lack of it), structure of the family unit, abuse, tracking records among mobile populations, acceptance into new communities, alcoholism and other substance abuse, friendlessness, self-esteem, Post Traumatic Delayed Stress Syndrome among veterans, affordable housing and medical care, societal attitudes, and physical and/or mental problems.

EXTENDING THE STUDY

Students might like to investigate the Community for Creative Non Violence (CCNV), the nation's largest shelter for the homeless and the closest thing to an American monument to homelessness. In 1984, Mitch Snyder, a homeless man, went on a fifty-one-day fast to protest the lack of national care for the homeless. As a result, the federal government made available to advocates the former Federal City College building at the intersection of 2nd and D streets in downtown Washington, D.C. This building, now called the Community for Creative Non Violence, routinely provides shelter for about 1400 homeless persons. As noble as it sounds, however, the CCNV is not without its critics, who say that it makes it too easy for the homeless to remain that way, that drug and alcohol use are rampant, and that it is unable to keep its promises, since it frequently has a waiting list and has to send homeless people to other shelters in the city. Students may want to compare the CCNV to Hull House.

CONNECTING TO LITERATURE

Numerous works of juvenile fiction dealing with homelessness have been published in recent years. Jerry Spinelli's award-winning *Maniac Magee* is popular with students and has available numerous kits and other prompts for use in whole-class instruction. Students might also enjoy reading and discussing Susan Dodson's *Have You Seen This Girl?*, Marilyn Sach's *At the Sound of the Beep*, Karen Ackerman's *The Leaves in October*, Gary Paulsen's *The Crossing*, Barbara Corcoran's *Stay Tuned*, Virginia Hamilton's *The Planet of Junior Brown*, and Susan Wojciechowski's *Patty Dillman of Hot Dog Fame*.

Maps

Purpose

As a result of completing the activities on this Bloom sheet, the students will demonstrate growth in the following areas:

1. locating places by showing absolute and relative locations;

2. demonstrating a knowledge of place and location by creating maps; and

3. exploring the relevance of geography as it affects life.

Knowledge: [Identify the following: political map, road map, graphic-relief map, weather map, chart, topographic map, natural resource map, and globe.]

Political maps use color to show countries and their borders. **Road maps** use color and other designations to identify roads, highways, expressways, and the like in a given area. **Graphic-relief maps** use shades of black or color to show the difference in the elevation of the land. **Weather maps** give facts about the condition of the air in a given place at a particular time. *Charts* are outline maps showing coastlines, water depths, weather data, and other information useful to mariners. **Topographic maps** graphically represent the exact physical surface features of a region. **Natural resource maps** show where things made by nature and used by people are found. Examples of natural resources are natural gas, timber, coal, water, and oil. **Globes** are small-scale models of the earth (or sometimes of other planets).

PUMP PRIMER ─────────────

Challenge more capable students to find other types—for example, dot maps, aeronautical charts, geologic maps, thematic maps, or population density maps.

Comprehension: [On a map, poster, or mobile, mount or draw an illustration of eight of the following physical features: canyon, gulf, lake, plain, river, strait, valley, peninsula, isthmus, fjord, delta, island, harbor, continent, mountain, and ocean.] Students who are not comfort-able with drawing may prefer to cut pictures from magazines. A supply of back issues of *National Geographic* is probably your best bet. If quantities are limited, consider letting students work in cooperative groups, reducing the need for resources. You might also check to see if your school or district has warehoused any outdated geography books; if so, perhaps your students could cut them up.

Application: [Make a detailed map of your school or of your neighborhood.] More capable students might prefer to make a model. Less able students need to work in pairs.

Analysis: [At certain times in history, maps have been considered so important that they were kept secret. List at least eight reasons why a map might be kept secret.] Answers will vary. Require reasons.

PUMP PRIMER ─────────────

If students are having difficulty getting started, you might mention ancient trade routes or military strategy maps.

Analysis: [Describe the differences and similarities between Mercator's map, Lambert's map, and fixed-point projection maps.] Answers will vary, but the key concepts include projection, representing a contour on a two-dimensional drawing, distortion, and scale. You'll need to decide how this information is to be presented. This might be a good time to teach or reinforce graphic organizers such as Venn Diagrams.

Synthesis: [Create and map a fictional continent on which you locate at least twelve different types of physical features. Use at least four features that were not listed in the comprehension activity.] The added features might include a pampa, an oasis, a plateau, a marsh, a prairie, a waterfall, an inlet, a sound, a channel, a cape, and so on. Have students extend this activity by exchanging maps and identifying the features on each other's map.

Evaluation: [Assess the advantages maps have over globes and vice versa. Give reasons for your answers.] Answers will vary. Consider such factors as storage, portability, cost, visibility, detail, distortion, scale, and size.

─────────────────────

The Newspaper

─────────────────────

Purpose

As a result of completing the activities on this Bloom sheet, the students will demonstrate growth in the following areas:

1. distinguishing between fact and opinion;

2. utilizing a variety of sources to obtain information; and

3. working independently and cooperatively within groups to accomplish goals.

Knowledge: [Name the sections of the newspaper. Describe the types of articles included in each.] Answers and work will vary.

It may be beneficial to bring in old newspapers, including issues from different days of the week. You may want to ask colleagues to bring theirs, too, or contact a delivery person and ask for a donation of back issues. If you are in a rural area, you may want to investigate the possibility of acquiring copies of a metropolitan daily. Other suggestions appear in the answer pages for the Political Cartoons sheet.

Comprehension: [Clip out two articles from the newspaper. Rewrite the articles in your own words.] Answers and work will vary.

This assignment is easily adjustable for ability or subject matter. It can be further defined by limiting the articles to your specifications. You may want to require one "straight news" article and one opinion article or editorial. Or, students could be asked to follow a story through several days' newspapers, to turn stories into a news broadcast, or to complete any of a variety of other activities.

Application: [Organize your own newspaper. Be sure to include the sections named in the knowledge task. Begin collecting sample features from the daily paper to include in your project.] Answers and work will vary.

As students look at the newspapers, have them note specialty sections that appear only on a particular day of the week, for example, Monday's business section, Thursday's foods section, Friday's weekend section, Saturday's religion section, Sunday's magazine—or whatever your particular newspaper includes. You may want to brainstorm reasons why a particular section is relegated to a particular day:

why not a Sunday foods section or a Tuesday magazine?

Analysis: [Select several articles from your collection to include in your paper. Point out the key facts in each.] Answers and work will vary.

Synthesis: [Publish your paper. Organize your articles so that your paper's format resembles that of a real newspaper. Create your own classified section. In the sports section, include a report about your PE class or a school team. Combine articles from your collection with the articles you create.] Answers and work will vary.

Evaluation: [Consider the statement, "I don't read the newspaper. Why should I? I can get the same information by watching the evening news." Decide if this is true and explain your reasons.] Answers and work will vary.

Political Cartoons

Purpose

As a result of completing the activities on this Bloom sheet, the students will demonstrate growth in the following areas:

1. identifying and interpreting a political cartoon;

1. questioning and hypothesizing about the role of the media in a free society;

2. evaluating the ethics and influence of political cartoons; and

3. explaining the impact of an individual on historical development.

Knowledge: [Collect five or more political cartoons.] You may want to decide in advance (and discuss with students) whether to include strip cartoons. Some popular cartoons (e.g., "Doonesbury") are routinely run on the editorial page in some papers. Though they are like comic strips in many ways (they feature fictional characters recurring daily, a serialized story line, and multiple panels), because of their political nature, a case could be made for calling them political cartoons. Such judgment calls are best left to the individual teacher. These activities are based on single-panel cartoons that are not serialized and that have caricatures or symbolic representations of real people and/or events.

Pump Primer

Some students may not have access to daily newspapers. To solve this problem for this and subsequent activities, you may want to collect the news and commentary sections from various papers and make them available to students. This can be simplified in a variety of ways:

- Ask your library or media center to save old papers.

- Post a notice on the faculty bulletin board making your need known, and provide a box for collection.

- Contact your local carrier and ask for donations of back issues.

- Ask your volunteer coordinator or other parent support

group representative to collect papers for you.

- Ask the League of Women Voters or other political organizations for help in collecting them.

- Allow students to use photo-copies of cartoons appearing in library books and encyclo-pedias.

- Allow students to photocopy each other's cartoons.

- Have students work in groups, so that fewer samples will be needed.

These papers might be saved for use with the Newspapers Bloom sheet.

Comprehension: [Write a one-paragraph summary of each cartoon. As you explain the cartoonist's message, be sure to allude to the cutline (title) and any other words used in the cartoon, the symbols and illustra-tions, and any exaggeration used.] Remind students that political cartoons are a form of journalism; thus all the examples may be appreciated on several levels. The fact that one person sees nuances that escape another doesn't mean that either is necessarily right or wrong.

Touch, too, on the differ-ences between fact and opinion: though political cartoons are usually based on fact, the main idea is generally just one person's opinion.

PUMP PRIMER ───────

Even if students are to produce these paragraphs inde-pendently, you and they might both profit from their being able to talk to one another. This

might be a good time to invoke the "three before me" rule, requiring a student to consult three peers before asking the teacher for help. Enforcement is crucial: asking Whom did you ask? What did they say? becomes a standard opening gambit for the teacher. You will benefit by reducing your workload, since you won't have to consult five times with every student. Students will benefit by being exposed to more than their own five cartoons, by having a variety of ideas to evaluate, and by having an opportunity to make decisions on their own. This method also validates the idea that kids can learn from one another while it provides a chance to shine for the student who is adept at analysis and insight but perhaps does not do as well with factual knowledge.

Application: [Choose an issue about which you have strong feelings—a classroom rule you disagree with or national policy or something in between—and sketch a cartoon to illustrate your position.] Responses will vary. Allow students to share their work. Point out that good political cartoons are self-explan-atory and that if something is unclear, it may need to be changed.

Analysis: [Find a newspaper story that has been treated both in straight news and in a cartoon. If you can find a related feature story, syndicated column, or editorial on the subject, include it. How do they differ? What facts are exaggerated, omitted, over-looked, or slanted by the cartoonist in an attempt to make

a point? Present your findings on a poster.] Responses will vary.

PUMP PRIMER ───────

Encourage sharing in some form other than an oral report; such as a poster, a chart, a scrap-book, or a bulletin board.

Analysis: [Research an influen-tial political cartoonist such as Thomas Nast, Bill Mauldin, Burt Tolburt, or Milt Morris. Share your findings with the class.] Responses will vary.

You will need to decide in advance how you want the research presented and to whom.

Synthesis: [Formulate a set of rules, principles, or standards that you think should govern political cartoons.] Responses will vary. However, the difference between telling a lie and omit-ting a truth is an important distinction for students to make: political cartoonists slant the news by giving only one side of it, not by giving false information. (This is a propaganda technique called *card stacking*, which is discussed more fully in the Bloom sheet on Yellow Journal-ism.)

Students should be aware of the three defenses used to protect the media in libel and slander cases: (1) the truth of the report; (2) the privilege of reporting (First Amendment guarantees); and (3) the allow-ance for fair comment and criti-cism.

Evaluation: [Decide which is likely to exert the most influence on the casual newspaper reader—a news story (or series of stories), an editorial, or a political cartoon. Justify your choice.] Any justified answer should be accepted. However, students should understand that political cartoons are a time-saving way of learning a little about an issue at a single glance, that they simplify and clarify at least some aspect of the issue, that they employ easily understood allegories that make assimilating new information easy, and that they are timely enough so that a person who hasn't read a paper recently can still gain a cursory idea of what's currently important.

CONNECTIONS TO OTHER SUBJECTS

Help students to realize that political cartoons may be about any subject, not just politics. Pool the students' cartoons and sort them by subject matter. Which ones are related to science? to current events? to music? and so on.

CONNECTION TO ART

Secure a local caricaturist or political cartoonist as a guest speaker. Display samples of the speaker's art.

ADDITIONAL RESOURCES

Hoff, Syd. *Editorial and Political Cartooning*. Stravon, 1976.

Honenberg, John. *The Pulitzer Prize Story*. Columbia University Press, 1959.

Keller, Marton. *The Art and Politics of Thomas Nast*. Oxford University Press, 1968.

Paine, Albert B. *Thomas Nast: His Period and His Pictures*.

Ayer Company, Publishers, 1978.

Peters, Mike. *The World of Cartoons: How Caricatures Develop*. Landfall Press, 1985.

Press, Charles. *The Political Cartoon*. Farleigh Dickinson, 1982.

Presidents and Their First Ladies

Purpose

As a result of completing the activities on this Bloom sheet, the students will demonstrate growth in the following areas:

1. demonstrating the ability to locate, access, organize, and use information;

2. determining the relative merits of individuals whom society has deemed important;

3. utilizing appropriate reference, study, and critical thinking skills to make decisions and solve a problem; and

4. analyzing how people create, utilize, and change the structures of power, authority, and governance.

Knowledge: [Make a list of United States presidents and their first ladies.] Such a list is available in many reference sources and textbooks, or you may wish to duplicate and distribute this one.

George Washington	Martha Dandridge Custis
John Adams	Abigail Smith
Thomas Jefferson	Martha Wayles
James Madison	Dolley Payne Todd
James Monroe	Eliza Kortright
John Quincy Adams	Louisa Johnson
Andrew Jackson	Rachel Donelson
Martin Van Buren	Hannah Hoes
William Henry Harrison	Anna Symmes
John Tyler	Julia Gardiner
James K. Polk	Sarah Childress
Zachary Taylor	Margaret Smith
Millard Fillmore	Abigail Powers
Franklin Pierce	Jane Appleton
James Buchanan	(never married)
Abraham Lincoln	Mary Todd
Andrew Johnson	Eliza McCardle
Ulysses S. Grant	Julia Dent
Rutherford B. Hayes	Lucy Webb
James A. Garfield	Lucretia Rudolph
Chester A. Arthur	Ellen Herndon
Grover Cleveland	Frances Folsom
Benjamin Harrison	Caroline Scott
(Grover Cleveland)	(Frances Folsom)

William McKinley	Ida Saxton
Theodore Roosevelt	Edith Carow
William Howard Taft	Helen Herron
Woodrow Wilson	Edith Bolling
Warren G. Harding	Florence Kling
Calvin Coolidge	Grace Goodhue
Herbert Hoover	Lou Henry
Franklin D. Roosevelt	Anna Eleanor Roosevelt
Harry S. Truman	Bess Wallace
Dwight D. Eisenhower	Mamie Doud
John F. Kennedy	Jacqueline Bouvier
Lyndon Johnson	Claudia (Ladybird) Taylor
Richard Nixon	Thelma (Pat) Ryan
Gerald R. Ford	Elizabeth (Betty) Bloomer
James E. Carter	Rosalyn Smith
Ronald Reagan	Nancy Davis
George Bush	Barbara Pierce
Bill Clinton	Hillary Rodham

Comprehension: [Design a game, puzzle, or maze that requires matching presidents to first ladies or requires knowledge of the sequence of presidential terms of office.] Responses will vary.

Application: [Choose one president and his first lady to study further. Compose a letter the first lady might have written to her husband during his term of office. In the letter, support one of his decisions or give reasons why you disagree with it.] Responses will vary. This is a good place to explore the influence of these women on their husbands and on the presidency itself.

PUMP PRIMER ─────────

This can be a good activity with which to close out the semester or year. Students could draw a president's name at random and then proceed. This method allows you to limit the activity to those presidents studied in depth and to monitor student accountability. If you wish to use this as a test, revealing what the students truly understand about the presidents and the issues they faced, you can require that the students rely solely on memory. If you wish to use it as an expansion activity, you can allow students to use their textbooks and/or to do research. In either case, you may want to combine this activity with the analysis activity.

Analysis: [Make one list of the attributes you think it is important for a president to have and another list of important attributes of first ladies. Check off the qualities present in the president and first lady you studied.] Responses will vary.

Synthesis: [Speculate how the roles of president and spouse will be altered when America elects a woman president.] Responses will vary, but students should probably be aware that some things that first ladies do are considered gender-specific and will probably be expected of a woman president until time and/or force of personality has produced a change in paradigms. The same could be true of some presidential roles, though that is perhaps a less likely scenario. (Usually, when women have begun doing "a man's job," they have been expected to do everything the men have done.)

PUMP PRIMER ─────────

Though the accomplished teacher integrates multicultural awareness informally throughout all instruction, this might be an especially teachable moment, a good place to stop and conduct a mini-lesson on gender bias. Typically, students at this age are much more gender-biased than they realize.

Evaluation: [Rank the top five presidents and top five first ladies. Disregard whether they were married to one another—you might choose Mary Todd Lincoln without choosing Abraham Lincoln, or vice versa. Give reasons for your choices.] Responses will vary.

CONNECTING TO ART/HOME ECONOMICS

The first ladies' inaugural gowns have been well publicized and can serve as an overview of how formal fashions have changed over the centuries. Students might like to sketch or make models of some of these gowns or to design a gown for a future first lady.

CONNECTING TO MATHEMATICS

Students should be able to easily gather numbers related to the presidents: age at election, height, years in office, number of children, and so on. These numbers could be utilized to figure averages, teach mean/median/mode, plot graphs, and accomplish other math-related tasks.

ADDITIONAL RESOURCES

Aten, J. *Presidents.* Good Apple, 1985.

Bain, R. *James Monroe, Young Patriot.* Troll, 1986.

Banfield, S. *James Madison.* Franklin Watts, 1986.

Blessingame, W. *The Look-It-Up Book of Presidents.* Random House, 1984.

Brandt, K. *George Washington.* Troll, 1985.

Collins, D. *Harry S. Truman; People's President.* Garrard, 1975.

D'Aulaire, I. and E. *Abraham Lincoln.* Doubleday, 1957.

Graves, C. P. *John Fitzgerald Kennedy.* Dell/ Yearling, 1984.

————. *George Washington.* Doubleday, 1936.

Melick, A. D. *Wives of Presidents.* Hammond, 1985.

North, S. *Abraham Lincoln: Log Cabin to the White House.* Random House, 1956.

Roosevelt, E. *Eleanor Roosevelt, with Love.* Dutton, 1984.

Sabin, F. *Young Thomas Jefferson.* Troll, 1986.

Santrey, L. *John Adams, Brave Patriot.* Troll, 1986.

Sullivan, G. *Facts and Fun about the Presidents.* Scholastic, 1987.

Sullivan, W. *Franklin Delano Roosevelt.* Harper & Row, 1970.

Sports Heroes

Purpose

As a result of completing the activities on this Bloom sheet, the student will demonstrate growth in the following areas:

1. perceiving events and issues as they were experienced by people at that time to develop historic empathy as opposed to present-mindedness; and

2. investigating careers related to sports.

Knowledge: [Cluster the following according to the type of sport the person is most noted for: Sonja Henie, Arnold Palmer, Joe DiMaggio, Jim Brown, Jackie Joyner Kersey, Henry Aaron, Ty Cobb, Joe Namath, Bobby Hull, Eddie Arcaro, Lou Gehrig, Bobby Orr, Willie Shoemaker, Willie Mays, Chris Evert, Jack Dempsy, Helen Wills Moody, Jack Nicklaus, Johnny Unitas, Babe Ruth, Muhammad Ali, A. J. Foyt, Wilt Chamberlain, Sugar Ray Robinson, Joe Louis, Ben Hogan, Bronko Nagurski, and George Mikan.]

Auto Racing: Foyt

Baseball: DiMaggio, Aaron, Cobb, Gehrig, Mays, Ruth

Basketball: Chamberlain, Mikan

Boxing: Dempsy, Ali, Robinson, Lewis

Figure Skating: Henie

Football: Brown, Namath, Unitas, Nagurski

Golf: Palmer, Nicklaus, Hogan

Hockey: Hull, Orr

Horse Racing: Arcaro, Shoemaker

Tennis: Evert, Moody

Track: Kersey

Comprehension: [Describe various ways of reorganizing the list of athletes.] Answers will vary but may include alphabetical order, men and women athletes, retired and active athletes, living and dead athletes, team sports and individual sports, contact and non-contact sports, sports involving a ball, and so on. If you wish to have students actually reorganize the list, consider printing the names on cards or on strips that can be cut apart and manipulated.

Application: [Collect newspaper articles, photos of present-day sports figures, and other sports memorabilia. Organize your collection into a "sports yearbook" or prepare a class bulletin board display.] Work will vary. You may wish to have students find information on the various Halls of Fame for baseball, basketball, football, and other sports.

Analysis: [Select a person you admire in the sports world. Determine if this athlete is a hero.] Answers will vary.

Synthesis: [Compile a list of qualities that would distinguish a person as a hero or heroine.] Answers will vary.

Evaluation: [Consider the world of sports. Decide which sport is the best and tell why.] Answers will vary.

Television

Purpose

As a result of completing the activities on this Bloom sheet, the students will demonstrate growth in the following areas:

1. oral skills;

2. analyzing the values and ideals reflected in television programming; and

3. identifying the importance of television in the lives of students.

Knowledge: [Summarize the principles on which television operates.] Depending on how you wish to have students obtain this knowledge, answers may vary widely in detail. Should you wish to present this information to students before asking them to summarize, the following data may be useful.

Television's workings depend on four principles:

Animation. The human eye retains an image even after the object has been removed from sight. Separate images seen at the rate of about ten per second tend to blend together. Therefore, it is possible to induce the illusion of movement by showing rapidly changing views of still pictures.

Emission. Certain substances are photo emissive:

they emit electrons when exposed to light. Others are phosphorescent: they emit light when exposed to electrons. Therefore, it is possible to convert light into electrical patterns at the transmitter and reverse the process at the set.

Segmentation. Images can be transmitted piecemeal and reassembled at the set.

Modulation. Radio carrier waves can be modulated, causing radio energy to alter its form according to a predetermined pattern. This is true not only of sound (as in radio), but also of pictures.

Television intelligence is transmitted via four signals: picture, vertical, horizontal, and radio. It is sent with 30,000 volts. It is segmented by 525 lines spanning the face of the tube on the horizontal. Each frame (complete image scanned left to right top to bottom) is transmitted in a ration of 3:4 (height:width) at a rate of 30 frames per second.

Comprehension: [Browse through a weekly TV schedule and make a list of the types of programs listed. Cluster these to form genres.] Answers will vary, but may include crime shows, dramas, situation comedies, westerns, police stories, talk shows, soap operas, variety shows, "infomercials," news magazines, gossip shows, educational programming, and the like. Depending on the maturity and ability levels of your students, you may wish to establish minimum, maximum, or optimal numbers of items on their lists.

Genres will also vary, and students may decide that some items are not easily classified. For example, some students might place gossip shows in a "true life" category with hard news and documentaries; others might put them in the same category as soap operas; others may decide they are a separate genre unto themselves.

Application: [Design a survey form and survey others about their viewing habits. Compile your results.] Answers and work will vary.

Analysis: [Compare a television news story with the newspaper coverage of the same event. Present your conclusions graphically.] Answers and work will vary.

Synthesis: [Draw conclusions about the concept of law and order in nineteenth-century America and again today by viewing a TV western and a modern police story. Interview a law enforcement officer about the discrepancies between what is seen on TV and what is actually happening on the streets. Decide how that probably applies to the western. Present your findings in an oral report.] Answers and work will vary.

Evaluation: [Choose a favorite TV program. Defend its characteristics as representative of or unique to its genre.] Answers and work will vary.

There's No Place Like Home

Purpose

As a result of completing the activities on this Bloom sheet, the students will demonstrate growth in the following areas:

1. demonstrating knowledge of place and location by creating a map;

2. explaining the impact of individuals, events, and trends on historical development;

3. examining the causes and consequences of people moving in and out of an area;

4. obtaining appropriate information from various sources; and

5. utilizing a variety of historical and contemporary sources such as written documents, oral tradition, literature, artifacts, historical sites, and photographs.

Knowledge: [Write a letter to the local tourism board or chamber of commerce requesting information on your area.] Answers and work will vary.

This sheet provides an opportunity for teaching an interdisciplinary unit with a language arts teacher. Alternative sources for information include a local auto club or travel agency. Usually this information is free. Data obtained for this Bloom sheet could be retained for use with the Field Trip sheet and vice versa.

Comprehension: [Draw a large map of your state or province. Fill in the map with names of cities, towns, waterways, historical sites, and other important features.] Answers and work will vary.

Application: [Collect information about your state or province. Select events from history, facts about famous people and places, and other newsworthy items. Present this information in the form of a travel brochure or pamphlet.] Answers and work will vary.

In order to counteract the "there's-nothing-to-do-around-here" syndrome, you might want to have students investigate free or inexpensive day trips. By setting a limit on distance or driving time (say, within 100 miles or a two hours' drive), you should be able to reinforce map, problem-solving, and math skills as students choose possible sites. Once completed, a master list could be duplicated for parents or used to plan possible field trips. Students might also explore possible weekend trips or "overnighters."

You may want to see if there is a local museum or historical society that would furnish a guest speaker.

Analysis: [Survey your classmates. Find out how many were born in your area, how many moved here from another locale, and how many anticipate moving away within the next five years.] Answers and work will vary.

Synthesis: [Make up a new name for your state or province. Design a seal and a flag and choose a motto.] Answers and work will vary.

Students may wish to see an example of the area's current seal, motto, and flag. Encyclopedias and almanacs are a good reference source. If your state or province has a handbook, students should become familiar with it.

Evaluation: [Consider the work of fellow classmates. Select the top five designs (from the synthesis task). Rank your choices, the first on the list being the best. Defend your decision.] Answers and work will vary.

CONNECTING TO MATHEMATICS

Have students graph the results of their surveys.

EXTENDING THE STUDY

Have a speaker from a local philately club talk to the class about the state or province as depicted on stamps. Students could then investigate the steps necessary for proposing a new stamp and could work together to submit a design. If you prefer, you could hold a competition to secure a design for submission.

Time

Purpose

As a result of completing the activities on this Bloom sheet, the students will demonstrate growth in the following areas:

1. identifying and applying appropriate time concepts;

2. arranging events in sequential order; and

3. analyzing the effects of technology on the global community.

Knowledge: [List five means or devices by which we measure time.] Among the means or devices students might choose are: the sun's "path" through the sky, the position of the stars, the changing of the seasons, the international date line, the meridians, sundials, hour glasses, clocks, watches, calendar segments (day, week, month, year), and so on.

Comprehension: [Illustrate five different time measurement devices.] Illustrations will vary.

Application: [Trace the development of the calendar and show your findings on a time line or flow chart.] Answers will vary.

Analysis: [Consider what clocks, calendars, sun dials, hour glasses, and star charts have in common and how they differ. Find a way to present your conclusions to the class.] Responses will vary.

Synthesis: [Invent a new device for measuring time. Explain its workings to the class.] Inventions will vary. In deciding on their inventions, students might enjoy learning about Rube Goldberg and his outlandish convoluted manner of accomplishing the simplest of tasks.

Evaluation: [Determine the consequences if suddenly the world were unable to agree on how to mark the passage of time.

Tell which three consequences would be the most sweeping and give your reasons.] Answers will vary.

Women in History

Purpose

As a result of completing the activities on this Bloom Sheet, the student will demonstrate growth in the following areas:

1. obtaining appropriate information from indices, tables of contents, dictionary entries, and other resources;

2. interpreting sources and examples of the rights and responsibilities of citizens;

3. investigating careers relating to civic responsibility; and

4. explaining the impact of individuals, events, and trends on historical development.

Knowledge: [Identify the following:]

Sojourner Truth: an orator who championed abolition and women's rights

Susan B. Anthony: a leader of the women's rights movement

Emma Willard: founder of Troy Female Seminary (1821)

Elizabeth Cady Stanton: a leader of the women's rights movement

Harriet Tubman: an escaped slave who led slaves to freedom in the north

Mary Lyon: founder of Mount Holyoke Female Seminary in

South Hadley, Massachusetts, (1837)

Elizabeth Gurley Flynn: labor organizer for Industrial Workers of the World

Lucretia Coffin Mott: women's rights activist

Frances Perkins: first woman cabinet member

Lucy Hobbs Taylor: first woman in America to earn a dental degree

Dorothea Dix: reformer who worked to improve treatment of the mentally ill

Jeanette Rankin: social worker and first woman to serve in Congress

Comprehension: [Summarize the need for equal rights for men and women.] Answers will vary.

Application: [Predict what life will be like for women in the future.] Answers will vary.

Analysis: [Research one of the women listed in the knowledge task. Write a report detailing her life and accomplishments.] Work will vary.

Synthesis: [Develop a skit that will demonstrate the changes in the lives of women from the past to the present.] Work will vary. These presentations may be done as pantomimes. Students should research the treatment of women through colonial times to western expansion. Students should be made aware of the changes in the status of women brought about by World War II. The skits need not be lengthy. They might be presented in the form of charades, in which other students guess the time period and the role being dramatized.

Evaluation: [Consider the changes in women's rights since the 1800s. Decide which advancement is the most meaningful to all women. Defend your answer.] Answers will vary. Women were given the right to vote in Wyoming in 1890. It wasn't until 1920 that the Nineteenth Amendment gave the right to vote all women. You may wish to have students argue for or against voting rights in a group discussion. The League of Women Voters chapter in your area may have guest speakers available.

CONNECTING TO LITERATURE

Have students read and discuss Eve Merriam's poem "Elizabeth Blackwell." Note Merriam's skillful use of word play to indicate gossip. Have students infer the difficulties faced by this young woman who in the 1840s became America's first female physician. Have them speculate on the strengths of character and personality that she needed in order to meet the challenge of realizing her dream. Ask whether they believe her difficulties ended when she graduated and have them elaborate on their answers. Ask whether there are any careers today in which such prejudices still exist. Then ask them to consider whether there are jobs where *men* encounter discrimination or prejudice because of their gender. Often transescent students do not realize that gender bias can affect either gender.

Writers Who Shaped History

Purpose

As a result of completing the activities on this Bloom sheet, the students will demonstrate growth in the following areas:

1. questioning and hypothesizing about the relationship between literature and history;

2. exploring the contributions writers made to the American political/historical scene;

3. examining how cultural elements such as gender, race, language, literature, and belief systems can both connect people and cause misunderstandings; and

4. constructing a time line.

Knowledge: [Construct a time line on which you place fifteen writers who shaped American history to 1865.] There is likely to be great variety in author choices unless you provide direction. For less able students, provide a list and ask them to arrange the authors according to the chronology of their most important works. You might want to include one or more writers from each of these categories:

THE PURITAN AGE

William Bradford	William Penn
Anne Bradstreet	Increase Mather
John Winthrop	Cotton Mather
Roger Williams	Jonathan Edwards
	Sara Kimble Knight

THE NEO-CLASSIC AGE

Benjamin Franklin	Philip Freneau
Patrick Henry	James Madison
Thomas Paine	John Jay
Thomas Jefferson	

THE ROMANTIC MOVEMENT

Washington Irving	Henry David Thoreau
William Cullen Bryant	Nathaniel Hawthorne
Edgar Allen Poe	James Russell Lowell
Ralph Waldo Emerson	Oliver Wendell Holmes

The anti-slavery movement offered numerous writers from across the time periods listed above, including:

Samuel Sewall	Jupiter Hammon
William Byrd	John Wollman
Phyllis Wheatley	Harriet Beecher Stowe

Arranging items on a time line is an exact science, with only one correct answer: work will vary depending on whether students arrange the writers by birth dates or by the date of significant works. Be more concerned with the technique of constructing a time line and with the rationales for placement than with specific order.

Comprehension: [Reorganize your list of writers to show which ones wrote about religious subjects, which wrote about historical or political subjects, and which wrote primarily to entertain. Determine where your time line can be broken generally into these three areas.] It should become evident to students that while writers may be listed under more than one topic heading, the earliest writers were concerned mainly with religious and historical matters; writers in the next group were concerned with historical and political topics; and only when these matters seemed settled did works written primarily to entertain emerge. This pattern seems to exist in the history of almost all literate civilizations and in the folk history of most other cultures.

Application: [Design a poster or use a graphic organizer to illustrate the connections between your writers and the historical events about which they helped to shape thought.] Responses will vary.

Analysis: [Choose one of your writers to research. Analyze how that writer's works influenced history and present your findings to the class.] Responses will vary.

Synthesis: [Compose a poem or story about a current social problem. Be sure to suggest at least one solution.] Responses will vary.

PUMP PRIMER

One way to encourage a broad range of topics is by doing a topic association web (or word web). Draw a circle on the board or in the center of a transparency. Inside the circle write the words "social problems." On lines radiating from the circle, write such terms as "science," "medicine," "politics," "entertainment," "the earth," "war and peace," and "religion." Students can help you generate the list. From each of those terms, allow students to suggest level two digressions and possibly level three digressions. (For example, from "entertainment," a level two digression might be "censorship." That might be further divided up into categories such as ratings for recordings and movies, laws against pornography, and parental veto rights.)

An alternate fluency activity is a cooperative learning technique called think-pair-share. In this activity, students are given a specified time to work alone to generate topics. (Two to three minutes is standard.) Students are then paired with a partner (use a triad, if necessary) to share items and try to double the number of items on their individual lists. If a new idea occurs to them, it should be added to both lists. The time limit should be increased only slightly, if at all. For the "share" portion of the activity, pairs are combined to make small groups and the process is repeated. A large group sharing can then be done to generate a master list, if desired.

Evaluation: [Decide which is most important in changing history: religion, politics, or literature. Justify your choice.] Answers will vary.

CONNECTING TO LITERATURE

Students often need help understanding that the early political and religious writings are in fact literature, just as surely as short stories, novels, and poems are—they are simply a separate genre required by the austere times in which they were written. More capable students might like to try the following analysis activity:

Stowe's *Uncle Tom's Cabin* and Paine's *The Crisis* both deal with social injustice and call for change, yet they are from very different genres. Learn about these two works and then speculate on how the historical time frame in which they were written influenced the author's choice of genre.

ADDITIONAL RESOURCE

Archer, Jules. *The Unpopular Ones.* Crowell-Collier Press, 1968.

ROOTS: BIBLIOGRAPHY

Bloom, Benjamin S., ed.; Max D. Englehart, Edward J. Furst, Walker H. Hill, and David R. Krathwohl. *Taxonomy of Educational Objectives, Handbook I: Cognitive Domain.* New York: David McKay, 1956.

Butterfield, Sherri M., ed. *Inventions, Robots, Future.* Santa Barbara, Calif.: The Learning Works, 1984.

Clements, Susan E., Kathy Kolbe, and Eleanor Villapando. *Do-It-Yourself Critical and Creative Thinking.* Phoenix: Kathy Kolbe Concepts, Inc., 1983.

Costa, Arthur L., ed. *Developing Minds: A Resource Book for Teaching Thinking.* Association for Supervision and Curriculum Development, 1985.

Forte, Imogene, and Sandra Schurr. *Science Mind Stretchers.* Nashville: Incentive Publications, Inc., 1987.

Gardner, Howard. *Frames of Mind.* New York: Basic Books, 1983.

Maslow, Abraham. *Dominance, Self-Esteem, Self-Actualization,* ed. Lowery. Monterey, Calif.: Brooks-Cole Publishing Co., 1973.

Meeker, Mary. "A Beginner's Reader about Guilford's Structure of Intellect." El Segundo, Calif.: SOI Institute, 1974.

Olson, Carol Booth. "The Thinking/Writing Connection." *Developing Minds: A Resource Book for Teaching Thinking.* Arthur L. Costa, ed. ASCD, 1985. pp. 102-107.

Reid, Charlotte, and John David Reid. *Soar: A Program for the Gifted Using Bloom's Taxonomy.* Austin: Pro-Ed, n.d.

Schurr, Sandra L. *Dynamite in the Classroom: A How-to Handbook for Teachers.* Columbus, Ohio: National Middle School Association, 1989.

Sizer, Theodore R. *Horace's Compromise: The Dilemma of the American High School.* Boston: Houghton Mifflin Co., 1985.

Treffinger, Donald J., Robert L. Hohn, and John F. Feldhusen. *Reach Each You Teach II: A Handbook for Teachers.* 2nd ed., rev. and expanded. East Aurora, N.Y.: D.O.K. Publishers, 1989.

Uhlig, Janie Mellecker, and Karri Jesson Ham. *All Booked Up!: Book Report Questions Keyed to Bloom's Taxonomy.* Laguna Niguel, Calif.: The Monkey Sisters, Inc., 1986.

INDEX

A

activity sheets
    grading, 9
    using, 7
African Americans, 81
Airplanes and Automobiles, 54, 130
American Cities, 55, 131
American Revolution, The, 20, 80
Americans with Disabilities Act, 140
analysis, 4
Annexation of Hawaii, 40
application, 4
Articles of Confederation, The, 82
Artifact kits, 113
assimilation, 87, 139
Attractions, 56, 132
Attucks, Crispus, 80

B

bandwagon, 108
Bass, Sam, 101
Bering land bridge, 15, 75
Bill of Rights, The, 82, 126
Billy the Kid, 101
Blackwell, Elizabeth, 153
Booth, Edwin, 95
Booth, John Wilkes, 95
Bowie, Jim, 89

Brown v. Board of Education of Topeka, 96, 126

C

Cabot, John, 77
California Missions, 23, 84
canals, rivers, and roads, 57, 133
card stacking, 109, 146
Careers, 58, 134
Cartier, Jacques, 78
Cavanaugh, James M., 86
CCNV (Community for Creative Non Violence), 143
Cherokee, 81, 86, 87
Chickasaw, The, 86
Chocktaw, The, 86
cities, 132
Civil Rights Act of 1964, The, 126
Civil Rights Movement, The, 51, 126
Civil War, The, 29, 93, 100
civilized tribes, 86, 87
Clark, William, 84
Clay, 88
Cochran, Jacqueline, 131
codes, 91
Cold War, The, 119
collage, 10
Columbus, Christopher, 16, 76
communication, 27, 91
Communism, 46, 117
Community for Creative Non Violence, 143

comprehension, 4
computers, 59
Constitution, The, 82
cooperative learning, 95
cotton gin, 103, 104
cowboys, 33, 98
Creek, The, 81, 86
Crockett, Davy, 89
cryptograms, 91
Curtiss, Glenn H., 131

D

da Verrazano, Giovanni, 77
data tent, 141
Davis, Burke, 81
Davis, Jefferson, 93
Davis, Richard Harding, 107
de Champlain, Samuel, 78
Declaration of Independence, The, 82
dime novels, 101
documentary (doc) stamps, 81
dove, 124
Duryea, Charles E. and J. Frank, 131

E

Early Explorers, 16, 17
Earp, Wyatt, 101
Eisenhower, Dwight D., 119, 124